To Ian and Elizabeth,

Thankyou for letting us take care of Far End, as mentioned on page 69 of this book. We hope you will be very happy in your new home. Come and visit us anytime.

lots of love

Ivan, Nikki & Freddie

CAMBERLEY

A History

CAMBERLEY

A History

MARY ANN BENNETT

PHILLIMORE

2009

Published by
PHILLIMORE & CO. LTD
Chichester, West Sussex, England
www.phillimore.co.uk

ISBN 978-1-86077-557-4

Printed and bound in Great Britain

CONTENTS

LIST OF ILLUSTRATIONS

Frontispiece: The *Cambridge Hotel* with Darracott's bread van outside in 1914.

ACKNOWLEDGEMENTS

The author would like to thank the staff at Surrey Heath Museum, Surrey History Centre, the Royal Military Academy Museum and The National Archive for all the assistance given to her. She would also like to thank Harry Goold and Margery Dowling for allowing her to copy extracts from the diary of their uncle, Frederick Street, and those who kindly allowed her to take copies of their photographs and postcards. They include Mrs Ida Andrew, Mr Graham Barson, Mr Malcolm Bowdery, Mr Chris Catchpole, Mr Ken Clarke, the late Mr Jack Croombs, the late Mr Mike Hawley (the *Camberley News* photographer), Mr David Howells, Mrs Shirley Koster and her brother Mr Gordon Pattenden, Mr Malcolm Miller, Mr Fred Penhallow, Mr Tony Wells King and Mr Michael Young. She would like to thank Eamon Ryan for proof-reading the text and Phil Stevens for making suggestions regarding the content of the book. She is grateful to the British Library for permission to copy the painting of the Obelisk, to Surrey Heath Museum for permission to use images from their collection, to Dr Thwaites of the Royal Military Academy for permission to reproduce a section of the 1809 survey of the estate, and to the *Camberley News*, whose reports and advertisements have been used throughout. She would also like to thank Ron Francis, for the use of his photographs and for his store of memories, so generously shared with her.

INTRODUCTION

The modern town of Camberley is built on a grid pattern laid down by an ex-Sandhurst gentleman cadet in 1860. The land was formerly heathland, waste of the manor of Frimley, which had been planted with fir trees after the Enclosure Act of 1801. These trees were harvested as soon as Captain Charles Raleigh Knight purchased the land and the 'new' town was laid out opposite the Staff College, which was built north of the London Road at this time. The town was zoned, with working-class housing and pubs nearest the entrance to the college and larger plots for the gentry in the surrounding countryside. The establishment of this settlement followed the pattern for the development of Yorktown (now merged with Camberley)

fifty years earlier, when the Royal Military College was built. Men were attracted to the locality, initially to assist in building the colleges and then to man them. With no large rivers to support industry and with very poor soil, the northern half of the manor of Frimley had been largely uninhabited and it was only with the work these colleges provided that the area developed. It was by no means an assured venture. Entrepreneurs arrived and erected a few dwellings before selling on, and with the bankruptcy of the first railway company Camberley had a very rocky start. This book outlines the development of the town from an open expanse of heathland, with a few dotted cottages, to the modern town seen today.

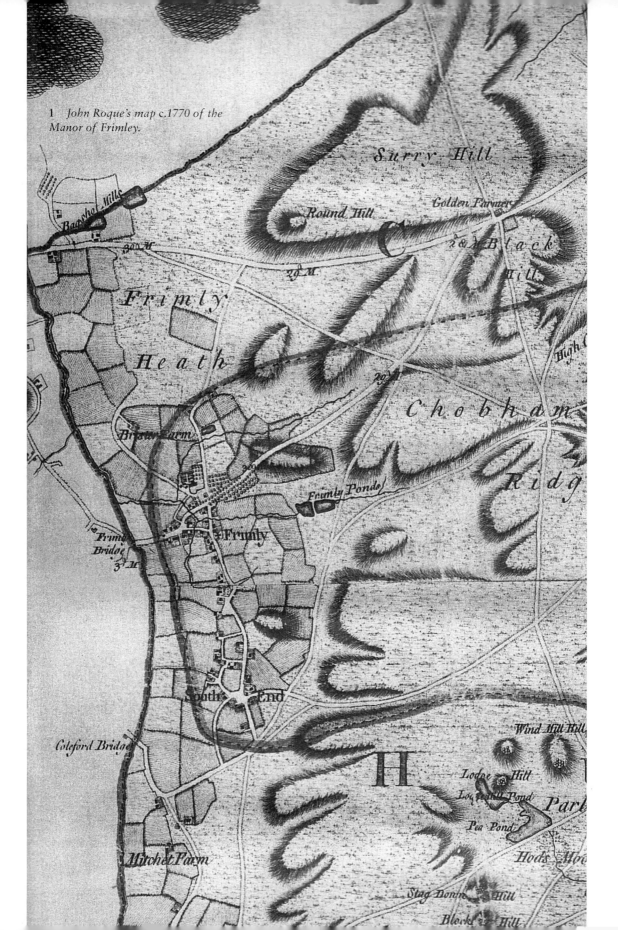

1 *John Roque's map c.1770 of the Manor of Frimley.*

One

FRIMLEY AND THE
ROYAL MILITARY COLLEGE

The land on which the Victorian town of Camberley was built consisted entirely of heathland on the northern edge of the manor of Frimley. A subsoil of Bagshot Beds and sandy topsoil made it largely unsuited to farming. There are no large rivers to support industry, just the Blackwater at its western border and the Wish Stream to the north. Springs rise on the higher ground near The Maultway, which permeate through the light soil falling towards the Blackwater valley. These form ponds, one of which, at Watchett's, still exists and a similar body of water once collected near France Hill.

There have been several finds of Stone-, Bronze- and Iron-Age artefacts and the remains of an Iron-Age hill fort. Known as Caesars Camp, it stands to the north of the town on the Roman Road, the Devil's Highway. There is some evidence of Roman activity, with finds of pottery and coins including Dr Stukely's reference in *Itinerarium Curiosum* (1724), to an 'urn with Roman coyns and itaglias'[1] found in

1710, and a collection of pottery unearthed at Whitwells Farm in Frimley Green in the 1990s.[2]

The name Frimley is derived from the Saxon 'Fremma's Lea' or Fremma's clearing in the woodland.[3] Frimley had been in Windsor Forest, which extended as far as Guildford. It is not named in the Domesday Book as it formed part of the manor of Henley (near Ash). It is said that the manor was given to Chertsey Abbey by the Saxon Azor for the 'benefit of his soul',[4] and with the dissolution of Chertsey Abbey on 6 July 1538[5] it was acquired by the Crown. Frimley Manor was held by the Crown until 19 May 1554 when Queen Mary awarded it to Sir John White. Lordship of the manor was then held by the Whites, followed by the Tichbourne family until 1789, when it was sold to James Lawrell. The manor extended from the Wish Stream, which forms the border with Berkshire and flows through the grounds of the Royal Military Academy, south to Mytchett Lake. The Maultway was its eastern border and the

2 *Sketch of Blackwater ford by an RMC Cadet, from a reproduction in the 1950s* Camberley News.

Blackwater River formed the boundary with Hampshire.

To the north of the manor was a mill at Blackwater, a few scattered cottages and a coaching inn, formerly know as *The Harrow* and later as the *Three Post Boys*, which stood near a toll house on the turnpike road.[6] The turnpike led from the *Jolly Farmer* inn, near The Maultway, towards Blackwater on a line roughly that of the London Road today. It was one of the main routes to the west and was busy with coaches and horse riders eager to get through a stretch of the journey considered hazardous due to highwaymen and the poor state of the roads. Two hundred years ago the only building of any note in what is now Camberley was the Obelisk. Built by John Norris of Hawley Place, probably as a 'view' or folly, it was erected in the 1770s high on a knoll of land that would have been visible from his estate[7]. It is believed by many to have been a signalling tower for sending heliograph messages to his friends the Dashwoods at West Wycombe, but there is no evidence to confirm this theory.

Frimley was a small village with a number of farms primarily along a ridge east of the Blackwater River, just west of the Frimley and Frimley Green roads. The number of inhabitants had remained fairly static for centuries as the land was poor, there were limited alternatives to farming for employment, and the population relied on heathland turf for their firing. In 1801 the population of the manor of Frimley was just 532 people living in 97 dwellings.[8] It was not until the construction of the Basingstoke Canal in the late 18th century and the

3   The Jolly Farmer Inn *at the junction of London Road and The Maultway, c.1906.*

Enclosure Act of 1801 that there were any major changes in the lives of the villagers.

The construction of the canal initially brought labourers and extra work for beershop owners, small shopkeepers and eventually bargemen and carters, and was one of the main reasons given for the purchase of land for the Royal Military College.[9] With the opening of the Wharf at Frimley Green in 1804, the first supplies of coal arrived and with it less reliance on the thousands of turves it took to supply each house with firing.

At enclosure the former heathland was apportioned to principal landowners and Fuel Allotments were set up at Frimley and Frimley Green to provide some benefit to the poor, who had enjoyed traditional rights to the use of the land. The major

beneficiary was James Lawrell jnr, a minor at the time, who had inherited the estate after his father's death in 1799. He was awarded hundreds of acres of land including that on which the town of Camberley was eventually built.

4   *The Obelisk, or Norris's* Whim, *painted by John Hassell in 1822.*

3

5   *Barossa Common, heathland devoid of large trees and owned by the War Office, 1912.*

The development of Yorktown and Camberley came about entirely through the building of the military colleges, the Royal Military, which opened in 1812, and the Staff in 1862. It was suitable due to its remote situation, 'being so placed as to avoid a neighbourhood injurious to the morals of the cadets ... [from many years of use of local land for] large encampments ... [and] the low price of land, with the vicinity of water-carriage by Basingstoke Canal'.[10] Those responsible for promoting it were the Duke of York and General Gaspard le Marchant. The land used for the Military College at Sandhurst, the old manor of Sandhurst, had been acquired by John Tekell in 1799 from the executors of Thomas Lodge. Tekell was about to marry Griselda Stanhope, the niece of William Pitt, then Prime Minister.[11] According to Phil Stevens,[12] as early as 1797 the War Office had identified this estate as suitable

for a college. There certainly had been interest in it earlier. In July 1788 General Thomas Cox wrote, 'I fear the Manor of Sandhurst is sold within these last five days ... the Purchaser is Described as a Young, Rich, Shooting Bachelor – who intends building a House immediately near Amborough Hill.'[13]

Thomas Liley was the man who occupied Sandhurst Manor until 1795, although there is no evidence that he purchased it or that he built a new house for himself, and for much of the time the overseers of Sandhurst had to visit him on several occasions before they could extract rate payments[14]. From 1796 until the sale of the estate to John Tekell it was let to William Collins Esq.[15] He paid rates for the 125 acre estate and Blackwater Mill although it is not clear that he lived in the house, as it was described as 'a shell' at that time by William Bray.[16] John Tekell

4

would not have had to pay a great deal for a small estate in a poor area of heathland. He had just resigned his commission in the army, following a short career in the 82nd Regiment of Foot, and it is said he used the money to buy the estate, although this has not been proven. What is known is that he was not wealthy. The Stanhope family did not wish Griselda to marry him, stating reports that he was 'a man of lost character, has spent all he has & sold the reversion of all he is ever likely to have, one sister married very low & the other of improper character'.[17] In a letter sent by Griselda's sister Lucy to William Pitt she asks whether she should tell Griselda or would he write to her himself. This was hardly the most propitious start for a niece

who was a favourite, so it is probable that Pitt 'allowed' Tekell to purchase the land knowing he would be able to sell it on at a profit.

Almost immediately after Tekell bought the estate Pitt purchased it from him. On 20 November 1800 Colonel Calvert, Adjutant-General, sent a report on the purchase of land to the War Department. The letter reads, 'a suitable piece of land has been found near Blackwater ... with a considerable quantity of Timber and some good Materials on the premises ... the Proprietor was disposed to enter into agreement to sell the same for about £8,000 ... the Board are of the Opinion that the purchase should be made without delay as the discovery of the object for which it

6   *Survey of Sandhurst Park estate in 1809 by Captain Todd of the Royal Staff Corps.*

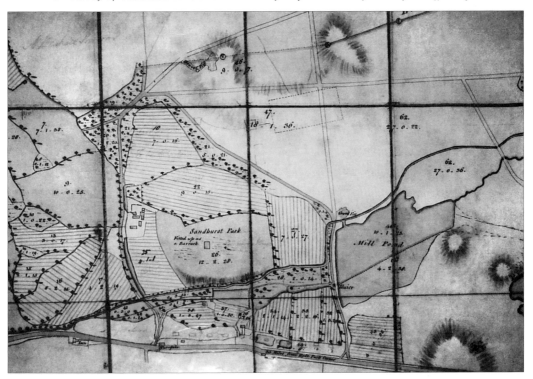

was wanted might induce the Proprietor to increase his demand'.[18] The proprietor was, of course, William Pitt and he was well aware of what it was required for. At the time he was busy supporting the plan for the erection of the College and proposing to Parliament that funds should be made available for it.[19] It appears to have been a blatant example of what we would term today 'insider dealing'. Sandhurst estate consisted of a manor house, farm and mill with 125 acres of enclosed land and 200 further acres of unenclosed heathland. A further 153 acres, part of Frimley Enclosure No. 1, was purchased by public auction for £1,560 in December 1801.[20] A contract with Alexander Copeland to build the College had been signed the same month and Edward Bracebridge moved on site to manage it and to lay out the fine grounds. In addition to the £8,000

paid for the main estate, a further £1,070 was paid in 1802 for fixtures and fittings which included furniture, farm goods and hot-house plants.[21] The final purchase of land, 11 acres bordering the north of the turnpike road between Frimley Road and Blackwater Bridge, was purchased at auction in July 1802 for £805.

The College was designed by James Wyatt in 1802, and immediately there were concerns about the cost. The estimate was for £118,956, which Wyatt felt could be reduced to just over £104,000 if they used Staff Corps and Waggon Corps personnel for some of the work. 'The enclosure of the Waste might be done by soldiers … during the summer months … in winter Trenching of Ground for Planting, clearing the Heath for cultivation, forming roads, etc.'[22] A list was made of suitable trades among men in Chelmsford Barracks. In 1803 the former

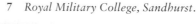

7   *Royal Military College, Sandhurst.*

8 *The Terrace at the RMC, built to house the Professors. It became known as Tea Caddy Row because of the shape of the houses.*

manor house was fitted up as a barrack room suitable for housing one officer and 100 men, at a cost of £1,072.[23] To cut costs Blackwater Mill was rented out to John Banks and there was an attempt to make bricks on site, but these failed. In 1806 they were perishing and were sold.[24] It is said the bricks were used to build the first of the dwellings in Yorktown, including the *Duke of York*. At this time, despite much money having been expended, there was little to show for it and there were those who proposed selling the estate. They included Nathaniel Kent, a government surveyor who valued the land at just £2,602. He felt it was uneconomic to build here, due to the situation far from any town, which necessitated building houses to accommodate staff.[25] College Terrace, or 'Tea Caddy Row' as it became known,

built to house the staff, were the first College buildings erected in Frimley. They were designed by John Sanders and the estimated cost of building them in March 1811 was £42,288, including the expense of transporting bricks from London. In 1809 the former manor house was fitted out for a home for the Governor, and the College Gate and Lodges at the Camberley end of the grounds were built in 1812. The cost of building the RMC was more than double original estimates and by 1816 Copeland alone had drawn over £243,000,[26] the total cost being over £333,000.[27] The first intake of cadets was in 1812. Lodges were built at Sandhurst, near Blackwater Bridge and at Yorktown in 1831, when an outbreak of cholera threatened to spread to the College.

9 *Yorktown Lodge, one of three lodges built along the perimeter of the College. A second was towards Blackwater and the third in Sandhurst.*

Despite setbacks and uncertainty, especially in 1806, it was on 25 March of this year that John Tekell, described as of Baringham Hall in Yorkshire, purchased much of the Frimley Park Estate from James Lawrell jnr.[28] This was just three months after the death of Pitt, but as Pitt 'owe[d] more than I can leave behind'[29] his death can have had no bearing on the Tekells' ability to purchase property. The estate included Frimley Park house and most of the land from Portsmouth Road to the northern boundary of the manor, excluding land from the corner of Frimley Road to Blackwater Bridge. Tekell paid £22,000 for the estate, making an immediate payment of £7,000 to James Lawrell. The remaining £15,000 has been the subject of much dispute and conjecture. Local historian Gordon Wellard wrote that Tekell obtained 'money bit by bit from his various friends, mortgaging to them portions of the estate as security for their loans'.[30] Another historian, George Poulter,

claimed the estate was lost by Lawrell in a game of cards, a story for which no evidence has been found.[31] In fact, it appears to have been a general land transaction where the purchaser, Tekell, could not pay all the cost of the estate without a mortgage.

In the churchwardens' accounts for 1806-7 John Tekell is living at Frimley House, as it is then called.[32] In August 1813, at a time when the future of the Royal Military College was more assured, he tried to sell the house, describing it as 'a Mansion with every convenience for a large family with fifty Acres of Land, in a ring fence'.[33] From a letter written in 1815 it appears there had been a move to rid the grounds of Frimley Park house of small cottages, enabling them to be enclosed. Griselda Tekell wrote, 'Mr Tekell wishing to get rid of the small cottages within the park paling has given a small piece of land in old Deane and one in [an] allotment next Mr Williams house to two persons of the names of Bains and Allen.'[34] John Tekell however was not without social conscience. When he found that Joseph Baines was an

10 *Frimley Park House, owned by James Lawrell and John Tekell.*

unreliable tenant, 'who was of dissolute habits, and would have soon parted with it', he granted the lease of the cottage to his son William 'at the rent of one pepper corne' for 999 years.[35] In all he gave nine leases of land in 1814-15 to poorer men, college servants, labourers and plasterers, and in the case of the Bains family he also provided them with the materials to build their cottage. He charged his tenants an annual rent of between 5s. and £1 10s.[36] He also had Whitehill Bottom Farm built, and these became the first houses erected in what is now known as Camberley.

In a document of 1813 attached to the Frimley Enclosure Award the two main land holders were James Lawrell and John Tekell. James Lawrell was living in Littlehampton at the time and Tekell was still, unhappily it seems, at Frimley Park.[37] It may have been that John Tekell, as Comptroller of the Mint from 1801 until 1847, an appointment in the gift of Pitt, felt Frimley was too remote from his work, or the upkeep was too much for him. In November 1815 they auctioned the contents of the house, which included furniture, wine, horses, dogs and 1,300 larch and young ash trees.[38] In the churchwardens' accounts for 1816, the house and estate are empty and the church rate remains unpaid.[39] The house remained empty until 1833 when James Lawrell lived there. Lawrell had been paying the rate on much of the land from 1824 while living at Farnborough Place.[40] It is unclear whether he was renting from Tekell or had just moved back in as the house had been empty for so long.

Lawrell was involved in the community at this time, becoming a churchwarden

11 *The entrance to Frimley Park House near the junction of Frimley Road and Portsmouth Road.*

from 1833 to 1836, an unusual position for the lord of the manor. In early 1837 Lawrell was still paying rates on Frimley Park house, but later that year Tekell was able to pay off the outstanding debt to him and he and Griselda returned to Frimley. He raised a dilapidation notice on Lawrell, complaining about the state of the house. It confirms that Tekell had made major improvements to the property prior to 1815. He complained that a stable for six horses and dog kennel he had built had been demolished, trees felled and 'the mansion … after Mr Tekell had been a short time absent was suffered to get in a most ruinous state. The Drawing Room lately built by Mr Tekell, the papering alone of which cost £40, was without windows and the cows got in.' He accepted that James Lawrell had 'laid out a large sum in … opening atticks, yet he cannot expect to be allowed for it, in fact his improvement having materially added to the expense of keeping it up there being about 20 additional windows'.[41] It leaves the question open as to who had the responsibility for the upkeep of the mansion between 1816 and 1833. Tekell clearly felt it had been Lawrell's. John and Griselda owned over 2,000 acres of land in the manor of Frimley in the mid-19th century but they did not become the lord and lady of the manor. James Lawrell jnr retained this title until his son, James Bathoe Lawrell, sold the lordship to James Fitchett Burrell on 25 June 1846,[42] having previously sold the southern half of the manor to Burrell on 21 March 1844.[43]

In the rest of the parish progress was very slow. In 1811 the RMC was still under

erection and the census confirmed that little had changed in Frimley. There were only 100 houses, an increase of three on 1801. There were 110 families, 14 of whom were employed in agriculture, 33 in trade and 63 otherwise employed. The ratio of males to females was high, a total of 427 in a total population of 702. John Tough, a local nurseryman whose premises were on the site of the present London Road Recreation Ground, took the census and remarked, 'It is evident that there has been for this few years past and will be for a good many years an increase in the

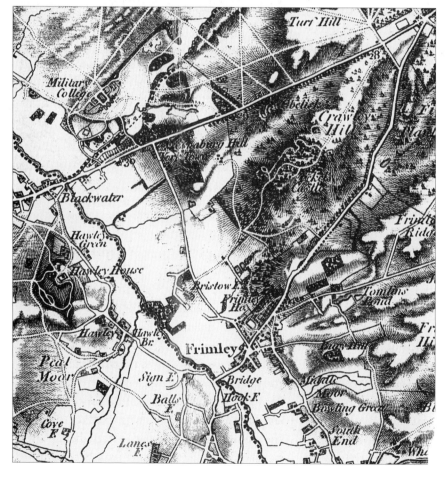

12 *Old Series OS map of 1816, showing the name York Town for the settlement near the new Military College.*

parish, which increase is Chiefly Owing to the Royal Military College, which is now Building near the north extremity of the parish ... it is understood that the College will remove from Marlow 1812 ... at a faire Calculation there will be at the End of 1812 Sixty houses built on this Parish since 1810.'[44] If John Tough was correct in his calculation it means that quite a few of the traditional houses were being destroyed and over sixty houses planned for the area we know today as Yorktown, including 26 in College Terrace.

It seems the figures produced by John Tough were considered unreliable as, unusually, a further census was carried out in 1815. The number of houses was then 210 occupied by 221 families. Each individual head of household was identified, probably so that no one could accuse the 'Minister, Chapelwardens, Overseers & other Inhabitants ... who hereby certify, that we have made a careful survey of the Population'[45] of making any errors. Forty-seven families were in farming, 55 were in trade and 119 were in neither. These included widows, those too old to work, gentry, and those who worked in the Colleges. The total population was now 1,107, 116 of whom lived in College Terrace, the remainder of the increase, almost 300 people, occupied houses and shops along the south side of London Road between Frimley Road and Blackwater Bridge and the west side of the top of Frimley Road. They were tradesmen who had set up in business directly opposite their source of income, the newly opened RMC and servants who worked there.

Yorktown was called New Town, Blackwater from 1804 to 1813.[46] Named after the Duke of York, who was Commander-in-Chief of the army when the College was built, Yorktown is first seen on the Ordnance Survey map of 1816. At this time it was a mixed settlement of

13 *The old National School, which opened in 1818. This is currently part of Trends Furnishing store, near the concrete elephant.*

shops, houses and public buildings. The *Duke of York* opened in 1816.[47] The first place of worship, a chapel in Frimley Road for Wesleyan Methodists, opened in 1807 and became a Baptist church in 1819.[48] The Frimley Church of England or National School opened in 1818, in a cottage opposite the RMC (a site occupied today by Trends furnishers), conveniently situated between the parishes of Frimley and Sandhurst for the Rev. Carwithen, then incumbent of both churches.[49] Yorktown was becoming

14 *Blackwater, looking east towards the railway line, with* The Swan *and* White Hart *on the left.*

a community but the remainder of the land towards Frimley and Bagshot was still predominantly heathland. It was also in decline as, in 1816, John Tekell left Frimley Park, James Lawrell was absent and, in 1818, £109 remained unpaid out of a total church rate of £231.[50] The partly 15th-century timber-framed chapel at Frimley was the only Church of England place of worship to serve the area. It had been patched up for centuries and was now considered too small for the anticipated increase in population. Opposing factions, newcomers in Yorktown and traditional residents in Frimley, fought over what should replace it and where it should be built. It is believed the Rev. Carwithen wished it to be built near Yorktown School. Eventually they chose to build next to the

existing chapel, and a fine local stone church opened on 18 October 1826.[51] The cost of St Peter's was partly defrayed by the publication of a sermon, preached during the opening service by Henry Austen, the brother of novelist Jane.[52]

The first railway station to open in the vicinity was at Farnborough in 1837 and until this time all travel was by horse, cart or the more comfortable carriage. The experience of travelling by carriage, however, was not without incident. In 1834 passengers alighting at Blackwater realised that the horses had 'found' their way to the hostelry without the coachman, who had fallen off some miles before.[53] There were also problems posed by RMC cadets. In 1833 three had climbed on to the back of the Southampton to London coach, and when removed by the driver had set upon him and the occupants. Raising a large group of fellow cadets, they had followed the coach to Bagshot. Here, at the *Kings Arms*, 'fifty to sixty of them, shouting and blandishing their bludgeons,' continued the assault.[54]

Blackwater had always been an oasis in a desert of heathland prior to the building of the RMC, and still offered decent alternatives to the growth in facilities at Yorktown. The landlord of the *Swan Hotel* in 1833 respectfully informed 'the Military & Gentry that the Fourth Blackwater Subscription Ball' would take place in April, when 'Lintoffs band will attend as usual'.[55] Blackwater was also chosen as the place to alight from the new railway line. On 8 October 1849 the Reading to Guildford line was fully

opened after controversy about the route it would take and how close to the College it would run.[56] The line was built nearest to Blackwater, as it was considered the alternative route closer to Laundry Lane 'would disturb the cadets' studies'.[57]

The only houses occupied in 1841 in the area known as Camberley today were those on John Tekell's land at Kings Ride, adjacent to the boundary of the RMC, and Ruby Doves, a substantial gentleman's residence known today as York House. It was owned by Alexander Morrison, then by Campbell Robert Cayley, an army clothier and draper, and later by the Over family who were also drapers.[58] The 1851 census named the area Mudd Town, an indication of just how lacking in identifiable features the area was. Despite the increasingly commercial

15   *Kings Ride looking north, c.1900. This was the first area in Camberley to be developed after John Tekell gave land here to tenants in the early 19th century for cottages to be built.*

16   *A painting of Pear Tree Cottage, one of the dwellings erected c.1815 in Kings Ride.*

nature of Yorktown, arable fields still abutted the rear of the shops and some farming survived. In 1849 James Boddy of the *William IV* advertised his 30 acre farm adjoining the public house.[59] Facilities were improving and the first receiver of mail for the Post Office was John Capner, appointed in 1844.[60] His premises were directly opposite the Yorktown Gate of the college. In 1851 his shop was surrounded by others offering stationery, tailoring and boot-making, as well as a barber and doctor. All manner of better-class residents lived in houses between the shops and hostelries along this one-sided high street facing the college, and the poor in the alleyways off it.

Living next to Dr Davis at Agincourt House in 1845 was the family of Arthur Sullivan.[61] Arthur's father took up a position as bandmaster at the RMC when Arthur was three years old and the family lived in Yorktown until 1857. It is believed Arthur attended Yorktown School until the age of eight. In later years he vividly recalled the murder of the Vicar of Frimley in 1850, and by coincidence returned to his old home in 1886, where he wrote *The Golden Legend*.[62] He did not forget acquaintances made in Yorktown and in his will left £50 to Lydia Thom, 'the daughter of my old friend Charles James Thom', a close neighbour of his.

Two

CAMBRIDGE TOWN AND THE DEVELOPMENT OF CAMBERLEY

John and Griselda Tekell, who died without issue, were buried at St Peter's and their estate advertised for sale. The first advertisement for their 'Residential Property with a domain of about 2,120 acres' appeared in the *Reading Mercury* in May 1858.[1] None of it sold. Whitehill Bottom Farm, with 77 acres, and Barossa Common, with 665 acres of land adjoining the Royal Military College, were purchased by the War Office for £4,500 on 26 April 1859.[2] This purchase included the single-storey cottages in Kings Ride. The remaining 1,457 acre estate, which included Frimley Park Mansion, Bristow and Axe Lane (Hack Lane Farm in Watchetts Drive today) farms, and a large tract of land with valuable plantations of fir trees 'with roads leading through and affording a forest scene ... a Castellated Cottage and an Obelisk placed upon the high ground ... picturesque objects amidst the dense foliage' were re-advertised in May 1859.[3] In the same month Queen Victoria inspected James Pennethorne's plans for a new Staff College to be built at the eastern extremity of the grounds of the RMC, near to the main entrance to the College.[4] These were then checked 'in every detail' and signed and approved by Prince Albert.[5] Designed to accommodate forty officers, the main interior feature, the entrance hall, was 'on the lines of a Roman bath, with passages leading from it the whole length of the building'.[6] Work began immediately under Colonel Chapman of the Royal Engineers, at the same time as the second auction of the Frimley Park estate, but the latter still found no purchasers.

In 1860 Captain Charles Raleigh Knight and his brother-in-law Major Robert Spring purchased the estate from Edward Newman, who had acquired it by private treaty earlier that year. As a former Sandhurst Cadet, Knight would have been aware of the possibilities for the development of the area. He had arrived at Sandhurst on 13 February 1827 aged 13 years, the son of Major-General Henry Raleigh Knight, and left on 31 December 1831.[7] He joined

17 *Painting by an RMC cadet of Yorktown c.1850, with the* Duke of York *and Frimley Road on the right, and St Michael's Church with scaffolding around it on the left.*

the 25th Regiment of Foot, became a Captain on 17 November 1837,[8] and sold his commission in 1844. Major Robert Spring, son of Lt-Col. William Collis Spring, purchased his commission in 1834 and sold it in the mid-1850s after winning a medal at Sutlej in 1846.[9] In 1850 Spring married Caroline, sister of Charles Raleigh Knight. When Knight left the army he went to Canada, where he became Superintendent of Military prisons. On his return to England he became Governor of Portland Prison, which opened in 1848, and Portsmouth in 1850. He was appointed Director of Convict Prisons in Ireland in the 1850s, where he joined a committee of three known as the Convict Prisons Board, responsible for setting up Mountjoy, Smithfield and Spike Island establishments. He married in 1856 and his son Henry Raleigh Knight was born in 1857.[10]

It is probable that Knight, used as he was to order and conformity, chose to lay out his 'new town' in a perfect grid pattern. The layout was further regimented by zoning, with cottages for the working class and their beerhouses nearest the entrance to the College and larger plots for sale in outlying regions. It is clear he wished to avoid the pitfalls of allowing narrow lanes of working-class houses to proliferate as they did in Yorktown. Numerous small alleyways leading south off the London Road in Yorktown had, by 1861 when the census was taken, acquired the most amazing if unglamorous names. Leather Lane and Screw Ball Alley may have described the trade carried out or the shape of the lane, but Dirty Place and Hovel Row could not have been desirable addresses and the need to avoid such street names in the new town would have been a priority. Knight's roads

16

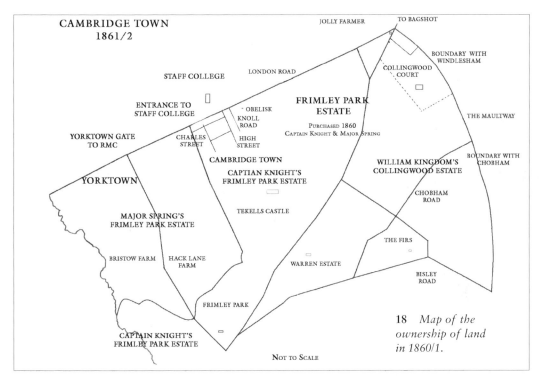

CAMBRIDGE TOWN
1861/2

JOLLY FARMER

TO BAGSHOT

BOUNDARY WITH
WINDLESHAM

COLLINGWOOD
COURT

STAFF COLLEGE

LONDON ROAD

FRIMLEY PARK
ESTATE

ENTRANCE TO
STAFF COLLEGE

OBELISK
KNOLL
ROAD

THE MAULTWAY

Purchased 1860
Captain Knight & Major Spring

YORKTOWN GATE
TO RMC

CHARLES
STREET

HIGH
STREET

BOUNDARY WITH
CHOBHAM

CAMBRIDGE TOWN

WILLIAM KINGDOM'S
COLLINGWOOD ESTATE

CAPTIAN KNIGHT'S
FRIMLEY PARK ESTATE

YORKTOWN

CHOBHAM
ROAD

MAJOR SPRING'S
FRIMLEY PARK ESTATE

TEKELLS CASTLE

THE FIRS

BRISTOW FARM

HACK LANE
FARM

WARREN ESTATE

BISLEY
ROAD

FRIMLEY PARK

18   *Map of the
ownership of land
in 1860/1.*

CAPTAIN KNIGHT'S
FRIMLEY PARK ESTATE

NOT TO SCALE

took names from local features. Knoll Road and Obelisk Street were named after the knoll of land on which the Obelisk was built, and Crawley Hill was a feature of the first Ordnance Survey map of 1816. Knightsbridge and Charles Street were named thus for obvious reasons.

In December 1861 it was reported that 'in the neighbourhood of Yorktown, within the past few months, building has been proceeding very energetically'.[11] Workmen sat down to a meal at the *Swan* in Blackwater provided by Knight to celebrate work carried out at 'Cambridge Town', the first noted reference to this name for the settlement. In the 1861 census there are no new buildings in Cambridge Town that are occupied, and the list of dwellings in the London Road finishes at the *Staff Hotel*, which opened in 1860.[12] But speculators

were aware of the potential, with 1,300 foot of frontage opposite the Staff College advertised in April as 'suitable for villa residences for which there is great demand'.[13]

19   *London Road, Yorktown. Before Cambridge Town was developed this was the commercial centre of the area, with shops and businesses lining the road opposite the College.*

On 21 December 1861 the *Reading Mercury* carried a long report on the death of Prince Albert, Queen Victoria's husband. It noted that 'towards the latter end of last month his late Royal Highness ... inspected the works [at the Staff College]; and it is feared he took a cold on the occasion, the weather being very inclement'.[14] The same week the *Mercury* reported that the College was rapidly approaching completion and was expected to be finished by March 1862. There were no reports of an official opening but in June, George Myers, builder of the college, sold off his plant and material by public auction.[15] The sale included brick-built offices, joiners, masons and blacksmiths premises, Bath stone, Portland paving and 500 tons of stable manure.

In October 1862 an evening of entertainment was organised for 'the Mechanics employed on the numerous buildings in the course of construction at Cambridge Town'. Provided for ninety men by Knight, it was hosted by his agent Langley Banks whose speech praised Captain Knight for the 'great risk he had run in speculating at the outset, on what could be termed nothing but a barren country [which] had been rapidly transformed, and villas, hotel, shops and cottages for the labourer could now be seen, and not

20   The Staff Hotel, *c.1900, with Harriett Young, the landlady, at the door. This was the first commercial premises in Cambridge Town, built directly opposite the Staff College to provide for those building the college.*

21   *The Staff College, which opened in 1862.*

only seen but inhabited'.[16] The event was held at the newly completed *Cambridge Hotel*. Captain Knight had taken a great risk. Men who purchased land from him were not always financially successful. The mortgagees of one speculator advertised his partially completed pair of semi-detached houses in April 1863,[17] and the following year one newly built house attached to a similar, incomplete one, plus several plots of land, and further unfinished property was for sale.[18] In 1867 Mr Brittlebank, having built some houses in Obelisk Street, was selling these and vacant adjoining plots[19]. It is not until 1870 that auctions containing more than one or two finished dwellings take place.[20]

A visitor in 1868 gave a vivid description of the RMC grounds which is in sharp contrast to the fledgling commercialism in the new town. It 'provides a scenery more like some wild Scottish district ... the college is situated on a rising slope in the midst of broken glades ringed with Scots fir, and underfoot on all sides, the poor messy ground is covered knee-deep with heather, where even now black game can be bagged, and the hen harrier seen quartering ... At the bottom of the slope a large sheet of water gives a bright character to the sombre hue of the heather and trees.'[21] Today this contrast between the bustle of town and the peace within the college grounds remains.

The ability to purchase, quite cheaply, large tracts of former heathland in which owners could create their own 'gentleman's estate' was attractive. The two founders of the town built large houses for themselves in extensive grounds on the outskirts of Cambridge Town. Charles Raleigh Knight lived at Frimley Park at the time of the 1861

22 *Tekell's Castle was built for Charles Raleigh Knight on the site of John Tekell's former hunting lodge in 1861/2.*

23 *Charles Raleigh Knight, the founder of Cambridge Town, strolling with his wife in the grounds of Tekell's Castle.*

census, but by the following year he had moved in to Tekells Castle, a castellated building erected on the site of John Tekell's former hunting lodge, and had let Frimley Park to Edward Pain.[22] Robert Spring was living with his brother-in-law at Frimley Park in 1861. He built Watchetts House, a Victorian mansion with gothic-style features, where he was residing in 1867, and rebuilt or remodelled the two farms, Axe Lane and Bristow. At Hack Lane, formerly Axe Lane farm, examples of these gothic features can still be seen.

They were not the first speculators to see the value of former heathland. Collingwood is today the name of a school and houses, and there has been much speculation about its local origin. There are those who believe them named after either Admiral Collingwood or the botanist Cuthbert Collingwood, or that it is derived from Colling Ridge, which is named on early maps. In fact it comes from Cuthbert Collingwood Hall, who was born near Newcastle Emlyn in Wales in 1809.[23] His father Benjamin Hall had estates in Wales and in Paddington Green.[24] They were a family of developers who built streets of houses for the rental market. In the mid-1850s Cuthbert Collingwood Hall acquired 750 acres of land bordered by Portsmouth Road (then known as Bagshot Road), Maultway and Bisley Road and known as Stake Bottom Heath and Cart Bottom Heath.[25] Here he started to build a mansion and set up an estate, naming it Collingwood Court. He died at Frimley on 17 February 1859, leaving property which included homes

24 *Watchetts House, a Victorian Gothic mansion built for Robert Spring.*

in Paddington Green, Great Yarmouth, Farnham Royal and Collingwood Court. He left Alexander Purvis, bailiff of his Frimley estate, 19 guineas and requested that his estate be sold.[26] William Kingdom purchased the unfinished mansion and all the land in 1860 for £5,500.[27] Kingdom, a former Clerk in the Treasury, sold 100 acres to Augustus Mongredien for his Heatherside Nursery by 1864,[28] and the partially built mansion to the trustees of the Royal Albert Orphan Asylum, where a national memorial home to Prince Albert opened in December 1864.[29] Kingdom built Collingwood Park off Portsmouth Road for use as his own home.

The Post Office Directory of 1867 gave an optimistic view of the development of the new settlement, possibly using information provided by Knight: 'Sunningdale and Cambridge Town Railway passes through, a station is to be in High Street'. It also said passengers and luggage would be conveniently connected to both the South Western and South Eastern lines. This railway, in which both Charles Raleigh Knight and Robert Spring were major shareholders, was a venture which suffered from major setbacks. In January 1862 there had been plans to build a tramway from Blackwater Station to Farnborough which was promoted by a Mr Cooper of London, and supported by Knight, Spring and Edward Pain.[30] It was Edward Pain, later of Frimley Green and Deepcut, who proposed that this tramway could be extended to include a 'street rail' to the *Staff Hotel*. Nothing further was heard of this plan and on 29 February 1864 residents rejected the proposed route of a railway from Sunningdale Station through Yorktown to Aldershot Camp in favour of a route via Bagshot to Cambridge Town and the London & South Western Railway station at Farnborough.[31] The promoters promised a further bill for an extension to Aldershot. An Act was passed on 14 July 1864, with capital of £70,000 to cover the cost of the line to Cambridge Town.[32] The first half-yearly meeting was held at the *Bell and Crown*, Bagshot on 17 October, when the contract for construction was given to Robert Taylor and engineer John

Ashdown.[33] In November, proprietors in the Sunningdale & Cambridge Town Railway met at the *Cambridge Hotel*, 'and with a fine wheelbarrow presented by Robert Taylor they proceeded to the end of the High Street where Mrs Jackson, wife of one of the Directors, cut the first sod'.[34] They adjourned to the *Cambridge*, where a hundred people celebrated the event. Taylor set up his yard at Bagshot, but cutting through sandy soil near the *Jolly Farmer* proved to be difficult. In early September 1865 three navvies were partly buried when sides of the cutting gave way, and the following month two further accidents occurred in the same place when a man suffered a broken leg and, later on same day, a carter was buried with several wagons.[35] Although no one was killed the accidents slowed down development. The company was declared bankrupt in 1866

25 The Cambridge Hotel *with Darracott's bread van outside in 1914. This hotel was built by Charles Raleigh Knight and opened in 1862.*

26 *The 1871 OS map of Cambridge Town.*

and on 10 March Robert Taylor's assets, which included a smithy shop, 8,000 oak, elm, larch and scotch sleepers, and stabling for 60 horses, were sold.[36]

The 1867 Directory also stated that Cambridge Town had 'sprung up' in the last four years and that about 200 houses had been erected, mostly convenient villas 'standing on their own ground of about two acres'. It claimed there was another 400 acres available for housing development at that date. The 1871 map would prove this was an exaggerated claim; although there were significant numbers of terraced and semi-detached dwellings for the working classes, there were few mansions. Royden Lodge and Heathcote had been built for Knight on the boundary of his estate at the junction of Park and Heathcote roads. In addition there

were The Knoll, Heathfield House and Hillside in Knoll Road, and The Glen, York House, Tudor Lodge, The Villa, Heatherley, Sutherland Cottage and Pine Tree Hill in London Road. In Portsmouth Road were Surrey House, Collingwood Lodge,

27 *Knoll House, the first of the houses to be built in Knoll Road, erected on a knoll of land below the Obelisk.*

23

Collingwood Court, occupied by the Royal Albert Orphan Asylum, and Collingwood Park.[37] The final three dwellings were Heatherbank on Church Hill and Heath Villas, a pair of large semi-detached houses which stood next to the railway cutting in Heathcote Road. There were also large houses in the High Street, a desirable residential area prior to the opening of the railway, but not standing in the two acres of grounds described in the Directory.

In addition there were a growing number of public facilities, including Knight's *Cambridge Hotel*, and the *Railway Hotel* which opened for business in 1864, despite the lack of a railway station. The *Prince of Wales* in Obelisk Street was licensed in 1862 and the *Brown Jug* in Princess Street

in 1867. In Park Street were two beerhouses, the *Ancient Foresters* and the *Carpenters Arms*, both named after the first industry in Cambridge Town, a sawmill in Park Street. When Knight purchased the land it was a fir plantation, all of which had to be felled before the town could be established. In November 1864 a Working Men's Institute was established, and that month 150 men 'sat down to tea in their large room'.[38] In April 1865 Cambridge Town Cricket Club had its first match of the season on Easter Monday, and later adjourned to the *Cambridge Hotel* for dinner.[39] Thomas Moth offered a carrier service twice a week to London, Walter Bartlett had his blacksmith's forge, and there were several grocers, a butchers and

28 *Park Street in 1907, with some of the first houses erected in Cambridge Town for working-class families. The row on the right, built in 1862 between* The Carpenters *and* The Foresters, *was known as Bank's Cottages after Langley Banks, Knight's agent.*

29   *Lawrence Stores, a large department store in Yorktown opposite Laundry Lane, had another store in Camberley and a warehouse near the railway station.*

a drapery shop. In addition there were the crafts associated with the building trade, stonemasons Adkins and Sumner, plumber Charles Warren, and Langley Banks, a landowner, builder and contractor. Banks was also agent for Knight and the first dwellings erected in the town were named Banks Cottages after him.[40] Yorktown, however, was still the bustling heart of the area, with 82 commercial advertisements in the directory against just 18 for Cambridge Town. Knight retained his hold over the latter, reserving the right to close off roads in the town until at least 1869.

Yorktown in 1867 was busy, not with huge numbers of large houses, but with an abundance of small dwellings for poorer residents and a large number of shops and

tradesmen. Larger houses included the Agincourt, Harcourt House, named after the first Governor of the RMC, Woodlands,

30   *Although land in Cambridge Town was owned by several small entrepreneurs by 1869, Charles Raleigh Knight retained the right to close roads.*

25

31 *The* Duke of York *offered the highest class of accommodation available for people visiting Yorktown. It opened in 1812.*

France Hill House, France Hill Villa (later known as The Whins), Park Villa (later The Poplars) and Watchetts House. Next to the *William IV* was a large pair of houses known as Sunnyside and Montague House. Yorktown also boasted a new gas works, which had opened in November 1862, four years after the formation of the company founded to run it. It had taken time to build but the delay was mostly due to a rival works in the RMC, which supplied lights to that establishment and to local houses. RMC gas, it was said, provided just a dull light and 'residents of Yorktown, Blackwater and Cambridge Town wanted bright light'. With this new supply 'the various shops and houses in the place were lighted up with gas for the first time this week, and over the entrance to the *White Hart Hotel* [Blackwater] a star of gas jets

shed forth a brilliant light in honour of the event'.[41]

In 1872 the LSWR deposited plans for a line from Ascot to Pirbright through Cambridge Town, with a station at North Camp. This would have adversely affected the South Eastern Railway, who objected to the proposal. On 16 June 1873 an Act was passed authorising the LSWR to build just over 11 miles of railway connecting Ascot with Aldershot, via Bagshot, Cambridge Town and Frimley.[42] Contractors were appointed in 1874 and work commenced using much of the route laid out in the 1860s. They had hoped to have the line open in 1877 but heavy winter rain in 1876 delayed the work. It eventually opened on 18 March 1878, with goods traffic commencing on 1 April.[43] The name Camberley was adopted on 15 January 1877.[44] Post had been straying to Cambridgeshire, and with the new railway station on the map another name was required. It was made up from three elements: the stream known as the Cam, which rises south of Old Dean on the London Road and flows through the town to the Blackwater (now piped underground), Amber Hill, a feature on John Norden's map of 1610, and 'ley', Saxon for clearing, as in Frimley and Yateley. The two local men responsible for the name were Dr Atkinson and David Sparvell, a grocer and baker who had arrived in the town in 1871 and eventually became an Alderman.

Initially a single line, the railway was widened from Frimley to Ascot and both lines were in use by July 1893. An accident badly damaged the Frimley Road Bridge in May 1893,[45] and on 10 January 1907 a locomotive reversing from the station

32   *The name was changed from Cambridge Town to Camberley by the Post Office in January 1877.*

33   *Camberley Railway Station photographed in 1914. The first trains passed through here on 18 March 1878.*

34 *Railway accident in Park Street in January 1907. After four days had been spent cutting away of part of the bank, seven engines finally hauled this one back up.*

35 *Camberley's first traffic jam. The flies, or fast carriages, were kept busy taking cadets and staff to the colleges. The building facing the traffic was the Police Station which opened in 1892.*

failed to cross to the up line and carried away stop buffers, sliding down the embankment in Park Street. The accident occurred just after midnight on Thursday when the train was empty apart from the driver, fireman and guard. Attempts were made on Friday and Saturday to pull the engine up the slope using two engines coupled together. The gradient proved too steep so part of the bank had to be cut away, and on Sunday afternoon, after coupling together six Drummond bogies and a tank engine, the locomotive was retrieved.[46]

By 1889, less than thirty years after the Staff College opened, the new town of Camberley had grown to a reasonable size, with a variety of shops along the London Road, High Street and the side roads. The population including Yorktown was now 1,882.[47] The range of goods available was increasing. George Snuggs, a fishmonger, and Robert Skerritt, who made watches, hairdresser James Haddow, dairymen Matthew and Thomas de Peare, coal merchant Thomas Martin and butcher William Wells were trading in the High Street. In Park Street was baker Thomas Powell, trading from a site later known as Wells bakery, and grocer Hannah Rummey. In Princess Street greengrocer Charles Cleeve occupied a site which later became a cycle shop owned by Percy Holloway. In Obelisk Street grocer George Axtell had his first shop.[48] There were still a large number of domestic dwellings in the High Street, including Silverthorn Terrace, which was known in the early 1880s as Lord's House because of the young titled men who stayed there whilst 'cramming'

36   *After the arrival of the railway the High Street became a commercial area. This view shows Collins store on the corner of Princess Street, Barclays Bank opposite, and the fishmonger's Armstrong. The fish shop was demolished in the 1970s and there is now a walkway through to Knoll Road.*

37   *Well's bakery in Park Street was open for business by 1889. It stood next to the alleyway from Upper Charles Street to Park Street.*

for Sandhurst at the Rev. Fox's school in Knoll Road.[49]

The prime site for businesses was still the London Road. Occupying the corner of the road at its junction with the High Street was a general shop and post office run by Charles Christmas, a branch of his larger premises in Yorktown. Adjoining were draper Thomas Fairey, cab proprietor John Hughes and butcher Walter Lambert. This was a business eventually owned

by Nicholas Verran. Henry Pank had his Emporium, offering to supply every household necessity, next to a small shop run by David Norman, who published the directory of the town in 1889 and became the Postmaster on 1 September 1890.[50] David Sparvell had his bakery next to stonemason Charles Adkins, and next to his yard was Camberley Dairy. Between here and the *Staff Hotel* were saddler Charles Evans, bootmaker Joseph Smallbone and ironmonger Henry Lunn. The last shops were jeweller Virden Cunningham, greengrocer Henry Maxwell and Thomas Armstrong's wet fish shop. Thomas eventually purchased George Snuggs' business in the High Street.[51] Most of these men lived in town for many years, using the profits from their retail businesses to erect dwellings for either the servant classes or to lease to army personnel.

38 *Camberley Dairy was one of many shops proud to supply the Royal Military College.*

39 *One of the first photographs of Cambridge Town, taken in 1873 of the corner of High Street and London Road opposite the Cambridge Hotel. It shows Charles Christmas's post office and general store.*

—— *Three* ——

CHURCHES, SCHOOLS AND THE URBAN DISTRICT COUNCIL

From 1851 residents of Yorktown were able to worship in their new church of St Michael, designed by eminent architect Henry Woodyer and built with local stone by William Kent.[1] It was funded entirely by public subscription, including a donation of £50 by Queen Victoria and Prince Albert.[2] The first, short-lived, incumbent, the Rev. P. Cornwall, did not attend any baptisms or burials. The first long-term vicar, Henry Percy Smith, was officiating minister by June, when he took the burial service of

40 *St Michael's Church, which opened in 1851, was designed by eminent Victorian architect Henry Woodyer.*

41   *Yorktown School in 1911. It opened in 1871 to accommodate 250 children.*

bootmaker John Stallwood who had moved to Yorktown with the College from High Wycombe in 1812. Like those after him, the Rev. Smith was often absent, and his duties were taken up by a number of men. The first baptism took place on 18 May 1851 when Stephen Ells, the son of shoemaker Stephen and his wife Maria, was baptised by James Trevitt, Vicar of Hampton.[3] The most memorable officiating minister at St Michael's was Charles Kingsley of Eversley, who conducted the burial service for General Frederick Rennell Thackeray, cousin of William Makepeace Thackeray, on 25 September 1860. Thackeray lived at The Cedars in Windlesham,[4] next to the church, but like many military men after him chose St Michael's as his final resting place.

In 1871 a new school opened next to St Michael's Vicarage. Known as Yorktown School, it was erected to accommodate 250 children. An appeal had been launched in 1869 for a new National School following the massive increase in population, 70 per cent since the previous census.[5] Estimated to cost £1,335, only £440 had been raised by April 1870. The Rev. Middleton tried to sell the old building but wrote, 'depression of the property, owing to the reduction of the Royal Military College, has diminished the saleable value of the site'.[6] There had been fewer cadets under instruction, but this had made little difference to the number of people arriving in the town, a fact borne out by the figures used to support a new school. Eventually the old school site was sold to John Lunn, an ironmonger, who built a shop frontage to the property still in use today as Trends Furnishers. The new school was officially opened by the Bishop of Winchester on 28 November 1870 and children moved in on 16 January 1871.[7]

Another school had existed in Plantation Row, Yorktown, as when Campbell Robert Cayley's estate was auctioned in 1872 it included a cottage which had been used as a school.[8] This may have been a British School for children of nonconformist families, given its situation, Plantation Row being known then as Chapel Place. In 1873 land was purchased in Obelisk Street and a small corrugated iron building erected for a combined Catholic school and chapel. Initially a chapel on Sundays and school on weekdays,[9] it opened in 1874 and by 1890 a more substantial building could accommodate 120 children.[10] Small children were eventually saved the walk to

Yorktown in 1889 when Camberley Infants School opened to house 120 pupils on a site in Princess Street. The school was extended in 1897, when additional buildings accessed from newly constructed School Lane were erected. This enlarged facility housed 260 children and was known as Camberley Mixed School. [11]

With the growth of the town it was time the spiritual needs of the residents were addressed. In 1874 land was purchased in Obelisk Street by the Rev. Middleton for the erection of a mission church to save residents of Cambridge Town their weekly walk to Yorktown[12] and Thomas Boys, of Frimley Hall, had a chapel erected

42 *St Tarcisius Catholic School in Obelisk Street, photographed in the 1950s by Ron Francis. It opened here in 1874.*

43 *St Paul's Church, built on Church Hill in 1902, was designed by William Caroe.*

opposite the entrance to his estate on Church Hill for nonconformists.[13] A report in the *Reading Mercury* in December 1881 described how 'a new Baptist Chapel has been erected at Camberley by Mr T. Boys at his own expense ... in the presence of a large congregation, the pretty little chapel being crowded. Many came from London and returned by special trains the same night.'[14] This building later became a mission church for St Peter's in Frimley.

St Paul's was erected next to the former chapel in 1902. Designed by Scandinavian architect William Caroe, it was built at a cost of £2,200.[15]

In 1892 St George's church was built in Knoll Road. It was intended as a memorial to Ellen Middleton, wife of the vicar of St Michael's. He had entrusted the design of the new spire of St Michael's to Arnold Hoole, as a memorial to his daughter Freda in 1891, and he had the same architect design the new church. Constructed of brick, in the Early English style, it was consecrated by the Bishop of Winchester in 1893.[16] The new spire of St Michael's and this church were erected by Norris & Sons of Sunningdale.[17] The original chapel of ease in Obelisk Street became known as the Obelisk Street Free Church. In 1909 a breakaway group from the Yorktown Baptist Church worshipped here and by 1915 had become members of the Congregational Union.[18] A new Methodist chapel had been erected on the

44 *St George's Church, which stood on the corner of Knoll Road and St George's Road. Designed by Arnold Hoole, it was built in 1892 as a memorial to Ellen Middleton, wife of the vicar of St Michael's.*

45 *London Road, Yorktown, with Victoria Avenue on the right. Beyond Victoria Avenue is Victoria House, the only tenement block in the area, and the* Kings Arms, *all owned by George Doman.*

corner of The Avenue and London Road in 1879, convenient for both Yorktown and Camberley, after a period during which members of the congregation had worshipped in a converted cottage near Agincourt House.[19]

With large numbers of wealthier residents there was a proliferation of private schools. In Yorktown in 1867 children could have attended Mrs Winter's or the Victoria School, situated behind the *Kings Arms*.[20] At Cambridge Town, Rose and Emily Eaton had set up the first Preparatory School at Heathfield House in Knoll Road. It opened soon after they moved to the house in the late 1860s, and they were still educating girls there in 1890.[21] There were a number of 'crammers' for boys wishing

to enter the RMC, including that attended by Winston Churchill in Knoll Road in the 1880s. In 1871 Rev. Cox at The Knoll had nine male boarders living in, between 11 and 17 years old.[22] This house, and Holmdale, were later owned by the Rev. Fox, a clergyman who also taught boys. By 1907 Mr Tinniswood had a school at The Knoll, and in 1914 Joseph Tinniswood moved it to Holmdale. It was to be expected that schools for boys entering the army would be located in town, but Camberley School in Park Street, situated where Pembroke Broadway stands today, was for boys entering the navy. Occupying a large house known as Pembroke Lodge, built on the site of the former sawmill, it had 15 boys aged 9 to 16 from as far afield as Queensland, the

Bahamas and St Lucia under the Principal, Henry Irving, in 1901.[23]

In 1901 the foundations of the first of two longer-lasting private schools had been established. Mary Cooke opened hers at York Terrace in Yorktown.[24] In 1907 Mary moved her school to Rossmore in Woodlands Road,[25] later moving next door to Fernlea when daughters Minnie and Joan took over. Known as Fernlea, it changed name after moving to a larger house, Lyndhurst, the name still used today. Elmhurst was established by Miss Amy Read in 1901 as a kindergarten over a shop in the High Street. It catered for children of army families. In 1908 Miss Marjorie Herring took it on and by 1914 it had acquired its current name

when she was joined by Miss Violet Crisp and the two moved to a house on the corner of Upper Park Road and West Road known as Elmhurst.[26]

There were other private schools. Beaufront, originally known as Maywood, was a girls' school established by 1904 in Maywood House in Portsmouth Road by the Misses Carr. Kingswood, later known as Cordwalles, Ballard and Wishmore Cross, was erected in 1901 on a site near today's Collingwood School.[27] Ernest Northcote, the headmaster, ran it as a boys' boarding preparatory school for those entering public schools or the Royal Navy. In 1908 fees were 100 guineas a year per boy and it boasted a well-equipped gymnasium,

46 *London Road, Camberley, with the Drill Hall on the left next to Yorktown School and Osnaburgh Parade on the right, in 1933.*

47   *London Road, Camberley, looking west c.1914, with the Post Office on the left and David Sparvell's bakery behind the parked car.*

a carpenter's shop and a dark room for amateur photography.[28]

In London Road in 1897 the Drill Hall was erected, primarily for training volunteer forces, although it soon became a hall for events as diverse as stage plays and adult education. In October 1897 a room was rented by Frimley UDC for technical education classes and lectures. Ten lessons in carpentry and joinery were offered for 2s. 6d. and six in home nursing for 1s.[29] In 1913 a new Methodist church was built opposite the Drill Hall, with funds raised by local printer and stationer John Drew.[30] After it opened for services the original chapel next to it became known as Central Hall; it was used as a church hall but other groups and societies could hire it, and this gave the town an alternative to the Drill Hall.

The first meeting of the Frimley Urban District Council was held on 2 January 1895 when 15 local men attended at a hall in Yorktown.[31] Councillors were a mix of local businessmen, George Doman, Edward

48   *The Wesleyan Methodist Chapel, which opened in 1913, on the right and the former chapel, which became known as the Central Hall, on the left. They stood on the corner of London Road and The Avenue.*

Over and Alfred Claypole, farmers, Rees Hall and George Hills, and military men, General Lempriere and Major-General Stotherd. In addition to these men were the nearest Camberley came to gentry, Dr Atkinson of Portesbery Hill, Herbert Hollings of Watchetts and Arthur Cadlick Pain of St Catherine's. Arthur Pain was voted in as first Chairman with Dr Atkinson as Vice Chairman. They discussed the appointment of a Clerk, Medical Officer of Health, Surveyor, Inspector of Nuisances and Rate Collector. A decision was made to 'take rooms as offices' in Silverthorn Villa at the top end of Camberley High Street. It was here that they met for the first time on 5 February 1895.[32] They were known as Frimley Urban District Council until April 1929 when the decision was taken to incorporate Camberley in the title.[33]

As soon as the Council was established one of its priorities was to improve sanitation and drainage. A new water supply was planned for Yorktown and Camberley to replace the well water which most houses relied on. This was to be provided by the Frimley & Farnborough Water Company, which had been established by Arthur Cadlick Pain in Frimley Green in 1893.[34] In the same year the Council passed by-laws regarding the keeping of pigs in gardens, purchased land for a mortuary near the railway line in Frimley Street and looked for a suitable site for an Isolation Hospital. Land was proposed at Barossa, Frimley Poor Allotments, Highland Farm, Old Windmill Gravel Pit at Frimley Green and Springfield Road. In 1899 a cottage in Gordon Road was used as a temporary hospital.[35] It was not until 1901 that a site in Mytchett (now Mytchett Recreation Ground) was purchased from Phillip Potter for £500[36] and a corrugated-iron hospital erected. There were six beds, four for scarlet fever and two for diphtheria patients.[37]

49 *Known as Silverthorn Terrace or Lord's House, this building stood on the corner of Obelisk Street and High Street. From 1895 to 1906 rooms here were used for Frimley Urban District Council meetings but in 1909 James Page converted the building into a department store.*

Almost every Sanitary Inspector's report contained complaints about overflowing privies and defective water supplies. In 1902 a report on the state of the sewers said little was salvageable, other than a new pipeline in Frimley Road. The proposed works would cost over £50,000 and it took many years before an improved sewage farm was built on land between Frimley Road and Blackwater River.[38] Facilities were also improving in other ways. London Road was kerbed with a wide pavement, men were employed to collect gravel from local pits for filling potholes, and roads were watered in warm weather. Watering to settle dust took place four times a day in High Street and three between Diamond Hill and Blackwater, all other main roads being done twice a day, over a distance of about six miles.[39] There was also a problem with litter, discarded fish and chip wrappers being a major contributor. Streets were cleaned each Saturday but residents on their way to church objected to litter from the evening trade, so Sunday street cleansing was introduced.[40]

The Victorian obsession with health was understandable when disease could strike at any time. In July 1878 Dr Augustine Barber Fry, who lived at Harcourt House in Yorktown, succumbed to diphtheria after visiting a patient.[41] In late 1886 there was a further outbreak of the disease in town. An official report in April 1887 stated that, 'Among the inhabitants of Camberley and York Town, estimated at about 3,000, the better class, military and civil, is strongly represented; but there is also a considerable population of cottagers and tradesfolk …

Diphtheria became last October suddenly epidemic in both places. On the 13th … a dozen or more cases … and in the next few days a couple of dozen fresh attacks … By the 24th October above 70 cases occurred and of these 13 had proved fatal … [It was] very early seen that all houses got milk from one source.'[42] All the children who died were from the upper classes of Camberley society. Among them was Elsa, the daughter of Dr Muller of Crosby Hill, Grace and George, the children of Captain Bethel Dawes of Osnaburgh House, and Hamilton, Kathleen and Mary, three of the five children of Dr Scott. It was held that milk supplied by George Hills of Park Farm was responsible. It was purchased just once a day in families who had staff and could store the milk, whereas poor families bought only enough for immediate consumption. Such storage in uncertain conditions was deemed to be the cause at the time.

A growing town needed a fire brigade and in May 1889 the Frimley, Camberley and Yorktown Fire Brigade was formed. The voluntary force kept a manual pump in a shed opposite the Drill Hall and horses hired from Mrs Young at the *Staff Hotel* were used to pull it.[43] Officers and fireman built their own station in The Avenue after borrowing £150 for materials. The foundation stone was laid in May 1901 by Mrs Hollings of Watchetts House and each person donating 1s. to the building fund had a brick inscribed with their initials built into the walls. The Police Station was built in 1892 and this became the headquarters for those officers searching for the killer of Mary Ann Hogg, whose body was found

50   *Members of the Frimley and Camberley Fire Brigade pictured in 1922 outside their station in The Avenue, with Herman Solomon on the extreme left and James Page next to him, two men who founded businesses in Camberley.*

by Colonel Lonsdale Hale on 11 June 1906. A Scotland Yard detective was sent to the town to assist in the investigation of the murder of Mary Ann, who lived with her sister Caroline at Heathfield in London Road. Local people believed Caroline was the culprit and this brought a flurry of reporters from daily newspapers to town. David Sparvell was foreman of the jury which decided there was insufficient evidence to say who committed the crime.[44] It remains unsolved.

In July 1904 the Rev. Middleton of St Michael's died leaving money in his will for a nurses' home. A meeting at St George's Hall decided a hospital was needed and Arthur Cadlick Pain became chairman of the fund to provide it. Several notable residents became involved. Mr Stone was appointed treasurer; others included Sir Arthur Hammond of Sherbourne House, F.J. Hurlock, manager of Simonds' Bank (now Barclays), Mrs Johnstone, the wife of Vice-Admiral Johnstone of Graitney, Rev. Kirwan of St Michael's, Dr Mounsey, Dr Scott and Mr J.F. Wright of Frimley Hall.[45] The foundation stone for the Cottage Hospital was laid on 12 December 1908

51 *Frimley Hospital in 1909, just after it was erected. Designed by H.R. and B.A. Poulter, it was extended in 1911 when wings were added to each end and a central doorway built.*

by Princess Christian, third daughter of Queen Victoria, and opened by her on 26 July 1909. It was designed by H.R. and B.A. Poulter and built by William Watson. The Poulters also designed the side-wing extensions in 1911. A ward was named after the Rev. Middleton, a bed was sponsored by Dr Rayner, and the operating theatre was dedicated to Captain Edward Davy Pain, eldest son of Arthur Pain, who was killed at the Battle of the Somme.[46] By 1929 the hospital provided 24 beds and two cots, the staff consisted of nine nurses and five domestic staff, and it was financed from a combination of patient's payments, subscriptions and charity donations.[47]

Street lighting in Camberley was by oil lamps until 1900 when those from Park Street to the Frimley Road were converted to gas.[48] The telephone service arrived in April 1897 and by August the National Telephone Company had received permission to erect poles between Camberley Station and Frimley Hall.[49] The

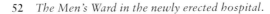

52 *The Men's Ward in the newly erected hospital.*

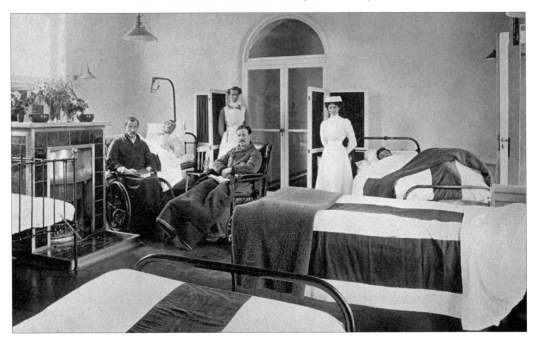

53   *London Road, Camberley in 1905, with Blairmore, the house and land purchased for the erection of new council offices, situated between shops in the foreground, and* Victoria Hotel *beyond the trees.*

first telephone exchange was in a house in Park Street near Wells bakery.

In 1903 a competition was held for the design of new council offices to be built at Blairmore, a house owned by Harry Doman which he was willing to sell for £1,350. Frimley Urban District Council purchased the property in September 1903 and the competition took place the following month.[50] Entries were given wonderful names: 'Hesperus' by William Hodgson, assistant overseer at Yorktown, 'Apercu' and 'Victis Honos' by Frederick Candy Uren, the Council's Inspector of Nuisances, and 'Pabulum' by H.R. and B.A. Poulter, which was the chosen design. The following February, no doubt upset by the

result, Mr Uren left to work in Aldershot.[51] Harry Reginald and his brother Briant Alfred Poulter were the two youngest sons of Bagshot Attorney Harry Poulter. They were born in 1879 and 1881 at the family home, Surrey House, opposite the *Jolly Farmer* in the Portsmouth Road.[52] After attending University College, Reading, they set up in practice in Camberley in 1902, submitting plans for the first of their houses, Collingwood Place on The Maultway, which became the family home. In 1907 their offices were on the first floor of what is currently the Old Thai House in London Road, a property which they transformed from a rather flat façade, with a slate roof, to the splendid timber-framed frontage seen today. They were well-known for using reclaimed materials and it is likely these timbers came from either Norfolk or Suffolk. They are best remembered for their beautiful Arts and Crafts style designs.[53] The council offices were erected by William Watson and opened by Thomas Forwood of Frimhurst in Frimley Green, then Chairman of the Council, in 1906.[54] Harry Poulter proposed that Blairmore, the original house, could be converted to a hospital, but nothing came of the idea and, apart from a newly formed bowling club using the lawn for a green, the house stood empty.[55] The brothers were responsible for the design of many local structures, including the Cottage Hospital, Camberley Heath Golf Club and Over's Store and warehouse.

54 *The timber-clad offices of H.R. and B.A. Poulter were situated above Permain Lyford, estate agents. This building was later known as Betty Brown's tea shop.*

55 *Frimley Urban District Council offices photographed in 1910, four years after they were built.*

56   *London Road Recreation Ground, with circular seating around the trees and its pavilion. The land behind the pavilion was not purchased until 1923.*

57   *Victoria Bowls Club members photographed outside their pavilion behind the* Victoria Hotel. *Seated in the bowler hat is George Doman and behind him can be seen the Council Offices.*

---— *Four* ———

LEISURE IN A GROWING TOWN

Despite the many calls on the fledgling Council's reserves it was progressing with new schemes to improve the town. In 1896 David Sparvell proposed that it establish a recreation ground in Camberley.[1] This was seconded by George Doman and in January 1898 Sadler and Baker, local estate agents, negotiated for the purchase of the land, formerly John Tough's nursery, for £1,163 3s. 4d.[2] A pavilion was erected by public subscription and Dr Muller donated plants and trees to enhance the grounds.[3] Further land was purchased from Mr Alexander in 1899 and swings and see-saws erected, but children broke the pavilion windows, cut their names in woodwork on a shed and damaged railings by swinging on them.[4] In 1923 Alfred Ives was paid £1,500[5] for land between the established recreation ground and Southwell Park Road and tennis courts, a rose garden and bowling greens were laid out here. The bowling greens were opened on 28 May 1925.[6] This was not the first bowling club in Camberley, Victoria Bowling Club, later known as Camberley

Bowling Club, having been established in June 1906, with its headquarters at the *Victoria Hotel*, which backed on to the park.[7] Their bowling green was on land behind the hotel and they played their first match on 8 July 1906.

In May 1901 it was suggested that an estimate be submitted for a bathing pool at the lower end of the Council's land at the rear of Yorktown Sewage Farm.[8] Later that month trial holes were dug on the site but no progress was made with the scheme. In 1902 bathing was permitted in the Blackwater River between 6a.m. and 8p.m. on weekdays, and from 3 to 8p.m. on Sundays. Rules and permits were prepared and one of the farm hands was employed to attend during bathing hours.[9] The facility obviously proved popular as in August men were sent to deepen the bathing area, although the water can hardly have been clean so close to the outlet of the sewage works. Councillors asked the RMC in 1903 if the lake could be used for this purpose but were refused as an agreement had already been made with the Post Office for

45

their staff to use it, and the Blackwater was used again.[10]

A cycling club in Yorktown, run by Mr Southey in 1889, is the first sports club of any kind to be noted in local directories. Camberley Wheelers' Cycling Club was formed by 1904, when members regularly held events in the Recreation Ground.[11] The club had to pay Frimley UDC a portion of its takings and restore the grass after each event. The Council also provided a tennis court and in 1906 the Regents Tennis Club had the use of it. By 1908 it was shared by the Alert Sports Club.[12] Frimley, Yorktown, Camberley and District Rifle Club was established by 1907 with Colonel Arthur Hammond VC as its president.[13] The miniature range in the grounds of the Drill Hall was open to members every Wednesday afternoon, plus summer evenings. Members also had the occasional use of a full-size facility in the Royal Military College. The first reference to an athletic event in Camberley was in 1904 when St Michael's Club booked the recreation ground for an 'athletic gathering' to be held on 13 July.[14]

Camberley Football Club joined the Surrey Football Association in January 1896 and won a first trophy in the 1897-8 season.[15] St Michael's and St George's both had teams at the time.[16] Initially they played in Mrs Mack's meadow in King's Ride, then on land off Frimley Road owned by coal merchant James Martin.[17] In 1905 their HQ was at the *Aspen Tree* pub and they were playing their matches on land behind it, part of the France Hill estate, which they moved from in 1909 when the property was sold. In 1906 the club was in financial

difficulties and almost folded but President David Sparvell found new funding and people to support it. In the 1908-9 season the Rayner Cup competition was founded by and named after Dr Herbert Rayner of Diamond Hill, to help fund Frimley Hospital. The event became known as the Hospital Cup. The Wright Cup, donated for the same purpose for senior teams, was presented by Mr J.F. Wright of Frimley Hall in 1913.[18]

There were several attempts to provide a cricket club in Camberley. In the 1860s there was a Cambridge Town team, but it is unclear how long this lasted. In 1908 the District Club, St Michael's and the Mess Staff at the RMC all had cricket teams, but there was no Camberley team.[19] Golfers had a choice. Barossa Farm Golf Club was formed by 1903 on land formerly part of John Craig's nursery, off Kings Ride. The sport was enjoyed by retired officers and Colonel Edward Wilson was Secretary in 1903 and Colonel Gwatkin in 1907.[20] Camberley Heath Golf Club opened on 1 January 1914.[21] The course, almost 6,300 yards long, was laid out by Harry Shapland Colt, who designed some of the best courses of this period and worked at St Andrews, Wentworth and Augusta. His fee for Camberley Heath was just over £72. The club house, designed by the Poulters and built by George Kemp, was demolished in the 1990s when the club was purchased by a Japanese company.[22]

Many leisure events were held in the college grounds: 'The Royal Military College Sports were held in May and were truly a local occasion and held on a Friday and Saturday; people from all around used

58   *A Foresters Parade marching down the High Street. The band is passing the entrance to Solomon's Garage.*

to attend. The main attraction was the Donkey Race ... the donkeys were tethered on the grass verge opposite Yorktown Post Office. From here the cadets bartered for their prospective mounts. Donkey owners from all round the district and Gipsies obtained anything from £1 to £3 for the services of their mounts and a good harvest was had by all. The race was held in fancy costume and the first prize was a hunting saddle.'[23] Annual Foresters Parades were held in the grounds of Government House which then processed through the streets of Camberley and Yorktown led by four mounted Foresters in field uniform.[24] But not all the overspill into town was welcome, and in 1904 a sham fight was held when rifles

were fired in streets near to houses, an action for which the army was held responsible.[25]

One of the best remembered occasions of the year was Rumble's outing, thanks mainly to the number of postcards sold of the event. Mr Rumble, who lived at Yorktown, had at first taken just his family on a trip to the sea, but later he devised a system whereby friends and neighbours could join him. He collected a penny a week from each person and in 1906 the scheme became known as the Camberley and Yorktown Excursion Club.[26] They visited Folkestone in 1907, 500 catching a special fast train at a cost of 3s. 6d., which included breakfast. They arrived at Blackwater station on converted coal

47

59   *Camberley residents waiting at Camberley station for a train to take them on a Rumble's outing to the sea. They include the builder Ernest Young and his family.*

and hay carts which had been boarded at Camberley at 4.30a.m. After breakfast many caught steamers to Deal or Dover, and after a busy but enjoyable time arrived back in town at 10p.m. In 1913 the final trip was to Portsmouth. They were not revived after the war.

Gale & Polden, publishers of the *Camberley News*, arranged to entertain the troops at Aldershot in 1906 with a 'cinematograph'. The absence of electrical current meant oxygen limelight was used to project the pictures onto a screen.[27] Camberley had to make do with something a little more standard. In 1905 Mr Chapman's portable theatre, which was made of wood

and large enough to hold 250 people, was erected at Doman's Meadow.[28] The Electric Theatre, Camberley's first cinema, opened in October 1910 in the High Street. Established by Mr Agar, who had cinemas elsewhere, with Alfred Ashby, a High Street draper, as one of the directors, it was opened by Arthur Cadlick Pain: 'Shows were one matinee plus two evening performances – a five-reel feature film would last about 1½ hours. Seats started at 3d., 6d. and 1s. in the war rising to 6d., 9d. and 1s. 3d. in 1922. Some local business people rarely missed a performance, notably Mr and Mrs Herman Solomon. Unlike in modern cinemas, the films were back-projected from behind the screen.'[29] Annie Mountford was the pianist, playing music to accompany silent films, and George Brett, who lived above the cinema with his family, the projectionist. A rival cinema was owned by George Doman. The Academy opened the Saturday before war was declared in 1914, having been built on the site of an old brewery next to the *Kings Arms* at Yorktown. It seated almost 500 people.

Other attractions included the Horticultural Society fete, held each summer in the recreation ground, and the Friendly Society Hospital Parade, which wended its way through the streets collecting funds for the Cottage Hospital.

One section came from *Anglers Rest*, Ash to Frimley Grove, one from Camberley station, and the third from the *Duke of York*. Along the way they would collect funds and then all would meet up on the Grove.[30] Sunday school, Empire Day and Coronation celebrations all meant the same thing for families in Camberley and that was tea, sports, baby competitions and fancy dress parades at the recreation ground, amongst the bustle and noise of the fairground. Whittle's Fair, with its gallopers, switchback and coconut shy, was a familiar sight, especially as their winter headquarters were just over the railway bridge in Blackwater.

60   *The* Cambridge Hotel *decorated for the Coronation of George V in 1911.*

Substantial mansions had been built to the south and east of the new town by the end of the 19th century and this growth continued in the early part of the next. The land behind Knoll Road and London Road, as far as Middleton Road, had been purchased by Edmund Atkinson. In January 1873 he wrote to Charles Raleigh Knight that his agent had looked at a piece of land near the Obelisk. Knight wanted £70 an acre but Atkinson offered £50 for each of the six acres. Knight replied that £70 'had been fixed some years ago ... but at present I am much more anxious about inducing a desirable class of persons to settle in our neighbourhood than I am about the actual price', and accepted the £50 price, a clear indication of how difficult it had been to encourage men to buy land here.[31] Atkinson built his own house, Portesbury Hill and Fosse Bank in London Road. He purchased The Glen, Heatherley and Sutherland in London Road, and cottages in Princess Street and Obelisk Street, all of which were let to tenants. In 1886 he had Cranmer Lodge built in Knightsbridge Road and in 1893 Sardensfield in Portesbury Road, both of which were also let.[32]

Crosby Hill, one of the largest houses built off London Road, was completed in 1886 for Dr Muller, who was born in Bavaria and came to England as private assistant to Warren de la Rue, maker of bank notes and postage stamps. He worked in the development of lithographic colour printing. A chemist by profession, he was a friend of Dr Atkinson who lectured on chemistry and physics, and it was probably Atkinson's influence that brought him to Camberley.[33] By the start of the 20th century nearly all the plots south of the road between the *Cambridge Hotel* and the *Jolly Farmer* were built on. One of the last, Woodcote, was an Arts and Crafts house designed by the Poulters for Edwyn Close in 1904. On the north side of the road York House and York Cottage, built in 1886, both opposite the Obelisk, stood in splendid isolation prior to Frank Bath's development of houses on the corner of Kings Ride in 1905. Towards the *Jolly Farmer* a few large houses had been built, including Cordwalles in 1900, which housed schools for much of its existence, The Grove, built in 1902, and Diamond Hill, designed in 1903 by the Poulters for Dr Rayner.[34] Housing development did not suit all. In December 1902 a letter written to national newspaper *The Standard* deplored the fact that 'Camberley has been covered by the jerry-builder with bricks and mortar' when its suitability for military instruction made it one of 'the finest and most useful spaces within 30 miles of London'.[35]

Portsmouth Road, as London Road, had developed primarily along the south side, much of the land to the north being one large estate, Frimley Hall. Thomas Boys, a London wine merchant, arrived in Camberley in 1878 when he purchased 240 acres of Collingwood estate, including Collingwood Park, from William Kingdom. The land bordered the Royal Albert Orphanage to the east, Upper Chobham Road to the north, a new road later known as Prior Road to the west, and Portsmouth Road.[36] At the same time Boys purchased land north of Portsmouth Road

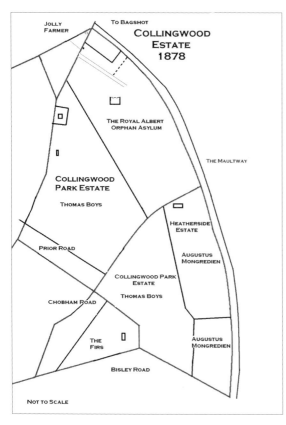

61 *Collingwood estate in 1878, when purchased by Thomas Boys. William Kingdom had sold off land to Augustus Mongredien, and a partly completed mansion to the Trustees of the Royal Albert Orphan Asylum.*

to Crawley Ridge and by 1879 had built a house there, initially called Hermon House, and then Swiss Cottage, but known today as Frimley Hall.[37] He erected two lodges in Portsmouth Road, one on Church Hill and one in Crawley Ridge. In 1884 prolific artist Richard Ansdell, who exhibited at the Royal Academy, purchased Collingwood Towers (Mulroy) from Boys, and died there on 20 April 1885.[38]

Between Frimley and Yorktown were Frimley Park and four houses built by

Robert Spring, Watchetts, Firwood, France Hill Villa and France Hill House. Frimley Park house and 142 acres of land had been sold by Knight in 1862 to William Crompton Stansfield, who died in 1874. His niece, Eleanor Herries, lived there until 1890. She retained ownership but the house was leased to a variety of tenants, including in 1898 the Crown Prince of Siam, Prince Vajiravudh, a gentleman cadet at the RMC who occupied one of the smaller attic rooms, protocol demanding that his servants and staff sleep below him.[39] It was purchased in 1920 by Theodore Alexander Ralli, who had been in trade in Liverpool. He was a keen agriculturalist and laid out a modern farm on the estate.[40]

Watchetts derived its name from the original 'woad scaet', or corner of land on which woad grew. These were field names at Yorktown when the Frimley Park estate was purchased by Spring and Knight. Major Spring sold the house to John Hollings, a Bradford man, who owned it from 1868 until 1884, when his son Herbert John Butler Hollings inherited it. In 1886 Herbert, or Squire Hollings as he was later known, married Nina, sister of the composer Dame Ethel Smyth, whose family resided at Frimhurst in Frimley Green. He had stables built in 1886, and two lodges, one in Park Road and one at the Frimley Road entrance, where the drive to the house had been planted with of row Wellingtonias. Squire Hollings died on 6 March 1922. His son had been killed in action in the First World War leaving his daughter Hildegard to inherit the estate. It was auctioned in 1922 and part was sold to

62 *The heavily wooded Park Road, looking north towards the town from the corner near Bristow Road today. This road formed part of the boundary of Watchetts Estate.*

a William Sowden, but the bulk remained unsold. This was purchased for £9,400 by Nicholas Verran, Camberley poulterer and fishmonger, in September 1924,[41] when it consisted of Watchetts House, stables, lodges and just over 180 acres of land.

France Hill Villa, built by Spring, was renamed The Whins and leased to a retired civil servant, Edward Hyde, by 1871. The house was on a ridge of land (now Robins Bow), with the heavily wooded France Hill estate behind and a garden falling away to the partly constructed railway line. In 1881 Hyde had vigorously opposed the setting up of a local board to oversee the now pressing issues of drainage and sanitary works and the upkeep of the roads, which was being promoted by James Burrell, lord of the manor of Frimley.[42] In 1889 Major

Samuel Rudge, best remembered for being one of the first men in the area to drive a car, purchased The Whins.[43]

France Hill House took its name from a feature on John Norden's map of 1610, which identified the former body of water to the south of the house as Pranzhill Pond, easily read as Franzhill. In 1877 Spring leased the house, standing in two acres, and adjoining Firwood House for four years to Lady Southwell, a widow. In 1879, after just half the life of the lease, she purchased them from him for £10,000, all of which he paid to Knight, to whom he owed money.[44] Lady Southwell's house was approached via a long drive off London Road (with a lodge on the corner of what is Grand Avenue today) which curved round to the house via a woodland drive between France

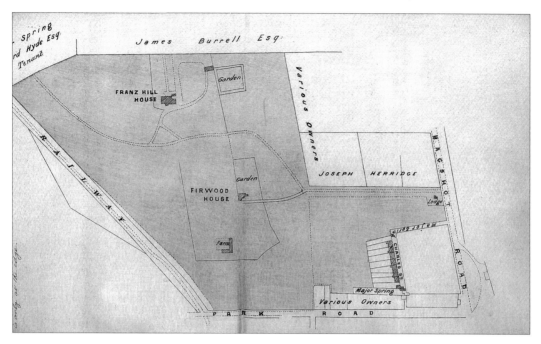

63   *France Hill Estate, still then known as Franz Hill, in 1867. The house was built by Robert Spring and sold to Lady Southwell. Bagshot Road is London Road.*

Hill and Firwood House. Lady Southwell was often away and France Hill was let for much of the time, but she was a benefactor to the Catholic Church, donating the land on which St Tarcisius stands in 1879.[45] Camberley's Catholic priest, the Rev. McKenna, lived in Firwood,[46] and it is likely to have housed successive priests until a presbytery was built for them in London Road in 1888.[47]

In Frimley Road, Harcourt House, near the *Duke of York*, was built for Dr Augustine Barber Fry in the mid-1860s. It was situated near the road, with parkland behind it which was often used for fetes and fairs and was later known as Doman's Meadows. George Doman, who was born in Basingstoke, came to Yorktown to work for Dr Fry as a groom.[48] In 1881 he

was landlord of the *William IV*. He set up livery stables at the rear of the *Kings Arms*, ran a two-horse bus service between Camberley and Blackwater Station and provided 'flys' or fast carriage services for the cadets. He was one of the first Frimley UDC Councillors in 1894 and was believed to be the first person in the town to own a telephone.[49] His interest in technology was put to public use when he opened local cinemas, the Academy at Yorktown and the Arcade at Camberley. He owned the only tenement block in Yorktown, Victoria House (site of Victoria Court today), and laid out roads from Victoria Avenue to Edward and Alexandra Avenue. Here he funded artisan's cottages, including the fine terrace at 1-23 Alexandra Avenue erected for him by local builder James Knight in

64 *Frimley Road in 1906, looking north towards Yorktown with the white entrance gates to Woodlands on the right.*

1903. In other roads he sold off plots for small-scale development. Doman Road is named after him, a small part of the land he owned for many years and where his ashes were scattered in 1940.

Doman's land was north of two earlier developments, Vale Road and Moorlands Estate, which both had buildings erected by 1882. Moorlands Cottage was built by Job Read in 1882 and Edmund Catchpole's four cottages in Vale Road were built in the same year.[50] Edmund and his cousin John, a carpenter, came to Camberley from Suffolk, married local ladies and built many local houses. Edmund's yard was next to William Christmas, the grocer,

near *The Crown* public house. Here he offered in 1889 to build a house, furnish it, provide warehouse facilities, sell you a piano and make your coffin.[51] To the south of Moorlands Road, the owner was Edwin Oades, an auctioneer and surveyor in Yorktown,[52] who laid out North, East, South and West Streets in 1894 on land purchased from Hollings of Watchetts House. In June 1914 these roads were renamed Queens, Burford, Brook and Oakley.[53] Eaton Road was developed by Edward Over in 1899.

On the eastern side of Frimley Road, Woodlands House, built in the 1860s and occupied in 1867 by Professor William

65 *Edmund Catchpole's yard in London Road, Yorktown, near Agincourt House.*

Walker of the Staff College, was the largest.[54] In 1879 Colonel Brackenbury lived there and by 1882 Walter Gee, the new owner, had sold off land between the house and the *William IV* for development. Oatlands and Lancefield were built in newly named Woodlands Road by 1882.[55] The status of this road, still considered one of the finest in the locality, was not affected by its proximity to some of the poorest addresses. Plantation Row and the lanes off it, built in the early 1860s for college servants and other workmen, were densely packed small four-roomed buildings. Many were originally owned by Campbell Robert Cayley and were sold

66 *The* Royal Standard *public house cricket team photographed outside the premises, with the landlord Harry Lovejoy seated at the centre with his daughter, in 1898.*

to local man made good, Henry Gray.[56] Henry, born in a dwelling next to the *Duke of York*, had numerous small houses built in Barossa Road and Kings Ride. He died in London in 1929 aged 99. After leaving Camberley he had set up a wine, spirit and grocery business in Buckingham Palace Road, initially as partner and then owner, and was an Alderman at the time of his death. He was well-known in Camberley as a 'conspicuous figure in his inevitable lavender trousers and white top hat'.[57]

built houses piecemeal, the lanes being named after them: Murrell, Goddard and Abbett. Watchetts Road, originally one of the drives to Watchetts House, was known as Tappings Lane by the late 19th century. Hope Cottages, built by Frederick Soan in 1891, were the first buildings erected here, followed by The Limes in the same year.[59] Between 1901 and 1907 almost all of Watchetts Road was developed, and in 1911 George Hoskins, a builder, had his house and yard established in the centre of it.

67 *Gordon Road, looking north. This distinctive terrace of three-storey houses was built by James Knight in 1899.*

Park Villa, later known as The Poplars, was built by Charles Raleigh Knight and still owned by him when it was let to Walter Gee in 1879, before he purchased Woodlands. It was later the home of Knight's son, Henry Raleigh Knight, who was instrumental in setting up a fund for the building of a mission church, a corrugated-iron building in Frimley Road dedicated as St Mary's in January 1904.[58] Between Park Villa and Watchetts Road were a number of small lanes where individual developers

To the north of the road are the rear gardens of Gordon Avenue, an extension of Gordon Road, which took its name after the death of General Gordon. This long road offered housing for all classes. In Upper Gordon and Middle Gordon Road are the largest houses, the exception being a row of worker's cottages known by the builder's name, Watson. William Watson, one of the most prolific builders in town, had his yard here and was responsible for building most of the houses in Upper and Middle

68 *Gordon Road, looking south from Park Road, with Gordon's Store and post office on the left.
This was converted to a house when a new store was built in Park Road in 1911.*

Gordon Road, which he sold or rented out to military personnel. Very large houses were built on the east of Gordon Road and between Gordon and Park Roads, and smaller detached and semi-detached houses were erected along the west side. In this road were three builders' yards: Frank Bath, at Durleston, Thomas King, who with his step-brother William Spear owned the company Spear & King, at Devonshire House, and

Mark Jacobs, whose father, a bricklayer, had built Belmont Mews, originally stables with tiny upper-floor rooms. These men were responsible for erecting most of the houses in the Gordon Road area.[60] The most impressive, Witwood, built in Park Street in 1898 for Major Crawford, was designed by the eminent architect Sir Edwin Lutyens. With its curved front walls and distinctive roofline, it is still an outstanding building.[61]

Five

OUTLYING ESTATES AND INFILL
DEVELOPMENT

On the outskirts of the town are a ring of estates. In Maultway the first house to be built was Yockley, designed by Reginald Bloomfield and built for artist Charles Wellington Furse ARA in 1899.[1] He had purchased the land from the Goldney family. Charles Wellington Furse, best known for the portrait of his wife on local heathland, known as 'Diana of the Uplands', was suffering from tuberculosis and was aware that the land, surrounded by pine trees, was good for his condition. In

69   *Yockley House was designed by Reginald Bloomfield and built for artist Charles Furse in 1899. When this photograph was taken it was the home of Walter Leaf.*

the short time that he lived here[2] his home was a magnet for other artists, including his friend John Singer Sargent, who was responsible for selling his paintings after his death.[3] In 1905 the owner of Yockley was Walter Leaf. The second house in the road, designed by the Poulters as their home, was Collingwood Place, erected in 1902, the first of three houses designed by them in The Maultway. The other two were Bagshot Heath, later known as Green Hedges, which was built in 1908, and Copped Hall, originally known as Maultway House, built for Colonel O'Shaughnessy in 1914.[4]

Heatherside was by far the largest estate. It was not the usual large house and grounds, but a large house surrounded by nursery grounds, avenues of select specimen trees and a farm. When William Kingdom purchased this land, in 1860, it was covered in fir trees planted by James Lawrell just after the Enclosure Act of 1801. These trees were now valuable and, as in Camberley, needed to be felled.

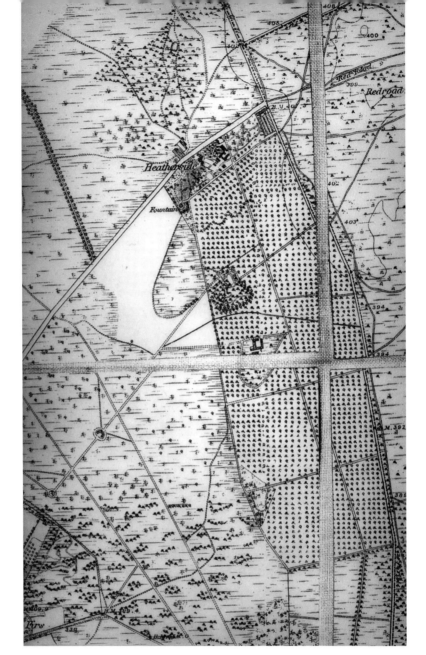

70 *The 1871 OS map of Heatherside estate including the nursery grounds and farm.*

There was an existing agreement between Cuthbert Collingwood Hall and Benjamin Hawkins to fell trees on the whole estate and to sell the timber, an agreement which stood until June 1862.[5] By 1861 the area had acquired the name New Zealand, an indication of how large the fir trees had grown, and Luke Locke, a sawyer, and his family were living there, along with two carters.[6] In the mid-1860s the land was purchased by Augustus Mongredien, a man with interests that included writing papers on Free Trade, playing international chess and experimenting with growing trees and shrubs.[7] He had Heatherside House built as a home and reception area for visitors, and the cottages on the corner of The Maultway for his workers. The avenue of

71   *Heatherside Corner. These four cottages were erected to house staff at the nursery.*

Wellingtonia trees, planted to provide a wind and frost break, is the only reminder of this nursery today, other than a few plants in private gardens.

After Mongredien's bankruptcy in 1875 the estate was owned by the Goldney family. The nursery was run by the Street family and Frederick Street jnr kept a diary of daily life here in the 1880s. In September 1886 he painted a picture of an idyllic lifestyle: 'Sunday spent by going in the waggonette to Yorktown Church, lovely singing – then around Frimley before going home.' The day before they had driven around the grounds of the RMC and 'in the afternoon and evening we had a long walk and then after tea music, singing and reading'. That Christmas 'I went to Yorktown ... and purchased all the little Xmas gifts ... we fulfilled the duties of Santa Claus and filled all the stockings with Christmas presents, wrapping the small

ones up in immense bandages of paper ... after this was concluded Alice and I set to work and gaily dressed the rooms with holly & evergreens and Christmas numbers of illustrated papers which made our little house seem wonderfully gay'.[8] It was not always so. In January 1887 he wrote:

We have still the wintry weather ... little can be done to enable the poor men to work as the snow is thick on the ground. A great gloom has been cast over us here at Heatherside this week ... I was met by Parker who came out to put our horse in when he asked if we had seen his little girl Emily and boy Archie as they had not come in to tea ... it seemed then to strike us at once that they had gone down to the half moon pond in the valley to slide and may possibly be coming from there now, Parker procured a lantern and we wended our way through the trodden snow in that direction at once with very excited feelings … as we neared the edge of the pond all was still as still could be when George turned the light of his lantern on the ice the deep utterance of heartfelt sobs and moans which at once burst from his lips as we could distinctly see where their poor little feet had been pattering in the snow sliding together for some time doubtless with the most gladsome excitement and then where they had turned to make a fresh slide on another part of the pond and alas! Fell through into the horrid cold water.[9]

After an inquest at the *White Hart* the children were buried at St Peter's in Frimley.

After the death of Frederick Street snr in 1906, Frank Stokes took over the farm at Heatherside, eventually opening a dairy in Park Street which he named Heatherside. In 1886 Thomas Reynolds, who had for a time rented Heatherside House, purchased land from the Goldneys and had a large house built known as Edgemoor. It was here that his daughter Grace invited her Sunday school boys to play cricket, and the games gave her the idea of forming a Cadet Corps in 1908 (which celebrated its centenary in October 2008).[10] On the western boundary of Edgemoor was The Firs. Built by 1871 and later owned by Edward Hyde Clark, it was occupied from 1895 until 1906 by James Graves. In 1907 Thurlow Astley, the new occupier, changed the name to Eastlea Court. It was demolished in 1935[11] and a smaller house was erected by George Hoskins.[12] It became best known as the home of Dr Barbara Moore, a Russian-born vegetarian, scientist and long distance walker who crossed America on foot in 1960. Next to The Firs was Edmonscote House, the site of Ravenscote School today.[13] Prior Place was built

72 *Prior Place Cross Roads, looking west, with the top of Prior Road on the right.*

73   *Baldwin Brown Convalescence Home was formerly Prior Place, the home of Prior Goldney.*

as the home of Prior Goldney in 1886, his Christian name being used for the house and road. In 1924 it was converted for use as the Baldwin Brown Nursing Home for recuperating patients of Kings College Hospital.

The name Tomlinscote is derived from the Old English 'Tom-ling' or common heather land, where commoners were able to graze their animals or cut turf for their fires. It was reached by walking up Field Lane with its common fields on either side. In May 1896 Hayward John Bidwell purchased the land from Richard Eve. It remained undeveloped until after 1902, when an auction of this land and part of Springfield Road was held at London. It comprised over 'twenty acres of beautifully wooded building land with an ornamental lake some five acres in extent'.[14] The

Tomlinscote land did not sell and by 1903 a ten-bedroom red-brick house was built for Mr Bidwell.[15] When sold by auction in 1924 some of the land had been used as a smallholding, or 'a small farmery' as described in the catalogue. There was stabling, a shed for cattle and a range of dog kennels and runs within the 22 acres of land.[16]

Alphington was erected in 1899 for Mr Edmund Furse (no relation of the artist Charles Furse) on land formerly owned by the Burrell family. In 1901 the estate consisted of the main house, stable and lodge. In January 1908 Mr Furse applied to have further stables built in Chobham Road. He died in 1918 in America,[17] where he had been a frequent visitor. Other houses nearby were Warren Farm and house[18] and Athallan Grange, formerly known

74   *Collingwood Crossroads, looking south up Prior Road from Portsmouth Road.*

as Oak Lea, built in 1892 for Emily Lyne and later occupied by the Spens family. These large dwellings had a remnant of the past in their midst. After enclosure of the heathland in 1801 Frimley Fuel Allotments had been set up to compensate the poor for the loss of their traditional rights. On the corner of this land (Tomlinscote playing field today) was the village workhouse. A small dwelling built to house those unable to work or house themselves, it was superseded by the Union workhouse in Farnborough in the 1840s. In the mid-19th century it was converted to two cottages, still occupied by the poor who rented it from the Trustees.[19] In 1901 they housed the Pearce and Collyer families.[20]

Charles Raleigh Knight, who built his Tekells Castle in fine wooded grounds on the outskirts of Camberley, had become 'squire' of a large group of employees led by his foreman George Hills. George, who was born in Mildenhall in Suffolk,[21] lived at Fern Cottage, which stood just off Park Road. His eldest daughter Keziah was born in Reading, where the Knight family lived before moving to Frimley Park.[22] Daisy, his granddaughter, recalled that George used to drive cattle to pastures along the High Street, just a track at the time, and let furnished property owned by Captain Knight, providing furnishings from a store held in Tekells Castle stables. When George's three children suffered from what was thought to be food poisoning in March 1868, Mrs Knight visited them and made an annotated sketch of the three children in bed. Tekells Castle Estate was put up for sale in 1869, when it consisted of 333 acres, many covered with fine trees including Deodara, Wellingtonia and Weymouth pines. There was an option to purchase additional land to the north, adjoining Church Hill and Crawley Hill. The dwellings for sale included Tekells Castle, with 12 principal bedrooms, Fern Cottage, a lodge on Portsmouth Road, three cottages further north on this road and newly built Oak Cottage (now the One Oak). There were issues regarding the sale.

Major Toke of Heathcote House had the right to walk in part of the woods and the main house had been let to Mrs Fitzpatrick until September 1875;[23] it didn't sell. Mrs Fitzpatrick was still in residence in 1871.[24] Knight eventually sold Tekells to Thomas Byrne RA and his Spanish-born wife Elisa in May 1882. They had been living in Woolwich and were at Aldershot from 1872 until 1881.[25]

75   *Mrs Knight's sketch of the Hill's children, Kezia, Hatty and Bertie.*

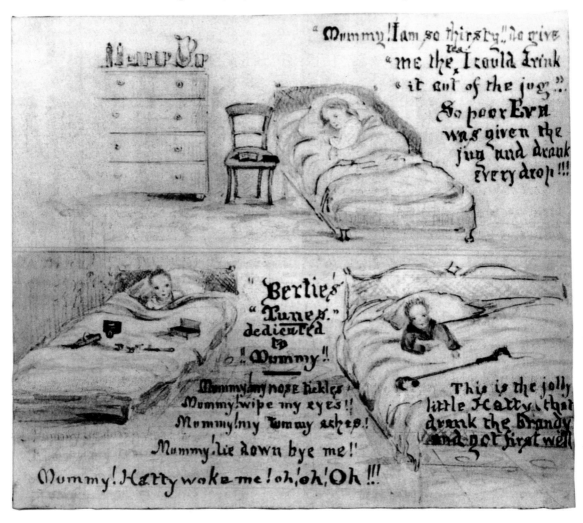

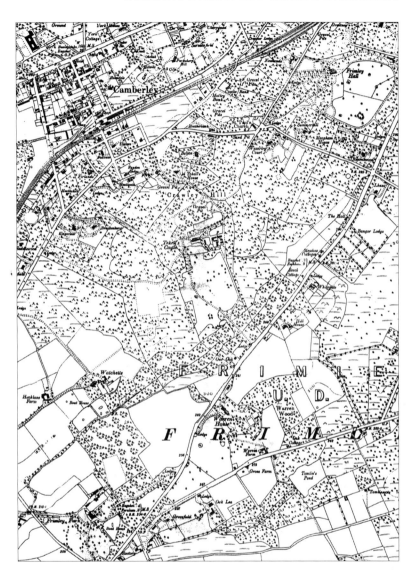

76　*The 1898 OS map of Camberley and Tekells Castle.*

In the mid-1890s Byrne sold off much of the northern part of his Tekells land bordering Church Hill. Prior to the sale there were only three houses in the area, Heatherbank House, Heathcote and Royden. Major Toke of Heathcote purchased 17 acres behind his house, creating an extensive barrier between it and future development.[26] Byrne named the land to be sold Pine Woods and Brackendale. Thomas Walker purchased Pine Woods, where in 1883 Belton was built as the home of Harrington Balfour.[27] His son Harold Balfour, later a Conservative MP, was born here in 1897. In 1887 Brooks Court, later known as Tekells House, was built.[28] The undeveloped land, including Waverley Drive and Belton Road, was sold in January 1898 by E. Walker of Parkstone in Dorset, possibly a brother of Thomas.[29] Brackendale was

65

77   *Church Hill, a postcard produced by local stationer and guide publisher John Drew in 1914.*

initially promoted by estate agents Sadler & Baker and advertised as the 'Archachon of England'. The brochure contained views of pine woods, grand houses, the College grounds and the canal and was sent to those serving abroad where it was thought

78   *Crawley Ridge, also by John Drew. He photographed many of the side roads not covered by national postcard producers.*

many homesick ex-Sandhurst cadets would take up the offer to purchase a slice of this idyll.

One of the first to have his home built here was Sir George Grierson, who lived at Rathfarnham in Pinemount Road. Although a maths student, he became interested in Sanskrit. He joined the Indian Civil Service and commenced his work as Superintendent of the Linguistic Survey of India in 1898; although the survey was completed in 1902, it was not until 1927 that all the books were published. Sir George was conversant in 180 languages and 480 dialects.[30] He and his wife were deeply religious, and Mrs Grierson founded the Ministering Children's League. Sir George died at Camberley in 1941 and is buried in an obscure grave in Frimley churchyard. In

79   *Sadler & Baker's offices on the corner of the High Street and Princess Street are on the left of this postcard produced in 1905 for Hankinson & Son.*

1898 Thomas Byrne died and by 1901 his executors, unable to sell, had let Tekells Castle to Miss Clara Faithful.[31] In July 1903 they managed to sell Tekells to Thomas Munro and John Thompson, who sold it on to Canadian Alfred Wilson Hughes in February 1904.[32]

At the top of Church Hill and Crawley Hill was Waverley Court. This house had been built on a corner of the Tekells estate in 1882 for Thomas Dyer Edwardes, who later became well known as a survivor of the *Titanic* disaster, his daughter becoming a heroine as she 'led her small boat through choppy seas, past icebergs and debris to the safety of the rescue ship'.[33] In 1901 Sir John Edge, who retired to Camberley after having been Chief Justice to the High Court in India,[34] owned Waverley Court. It was an

oasis of peace surrounded by a permanent building site. The Waverley Court Estate Company, incorporated in August 1899, purchased the remaining land put up for sale by Walker in 1898, plus land between Waverley Court and Portsmouth Road.

80   *Waverley Court, one of the largest mansions in Camberley.*

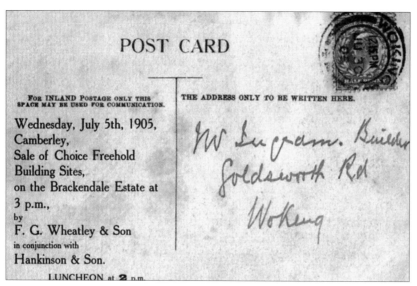

POST CARD

FOR INLAND POSTAGE ONLY THIS
SPACE MAY BE USED FOR COMMUNICATION.

Wednesday, July 5th, 1905,
Camberley,
Sale of Choice Freehold
Building Sites,
on the Brackendale Estate at
3 p.m.,
by
F. G. Wheatley & Son
in conjunction with
Hankinson & Son.

LUNCHEON at 2 p.m.

THE ADDRESS ONLY TO BE WRITTEN HERE.

*Mr Ingram. Builder
Goldsworth Rd
Woking*

81 *Reverse of the 1905 postcard sent to builders to encourage them to purchase land at Brackendale.*

This group of men, who it is said had built many fine houses in Bournemouth, were now keen to build in Camberley. They were estate agents Thomas and Francis Hankinson, architects George Lawson and William Reynolds, and builders Edwin Bath and Thomas Penton.[35] The company was set up with £10,000 of capital, which was increased to £15,000 in 1903 when Alfred Wilson Hughes, later of Tekells Castle, bought into the venture.[36] Waverley, Connaught and Castle Roads were laid out and the first of the houses designed by Lawson and Reynolds were built: Danesfort in 1900; Lammermoor, later known as Rockhurst, in 1901 in Waverley Drive; Thornton, also known as Thackeray, in 1901 in Castle Road, and Craigleith, later Moynalty, in Connaught Road.[37]

Although two builders were share-holders it was another builder, Levi Hammerton, originally of Holdenhurst near Bournemouth, who erected most of the houses here between 1900 and 1908.[38] Edwin Bath and Thomas Penton may have

fallen foul of the regulations relating to building properties in Camberley. They were charged with building without proper foundations, not having enough height in rooms, and not submitting new plans when the first had been rejected.[39] The same group of men, including Alfred Wilson Hughes, had purchased Brackendale Estate from Sadler and Baker and by 1903 were erecting houses designed by Lawson and Reynolds, including Beechleigh, Brackendale, Medley and Dormer Cottages and Minden and The Nook. Hughes sold the land between Tekells Castle, which had been destroyed by an explosion and fire during the night of 5 October 1906, and Park Road, now known as Tekels Avenue, to John Ashby in May 1909. Builders from outside the area were invited to view the area's potential in 1905, but plots were slow to sell, and the Waverley Court Company was still advertising building land between Belton Road and Portsmouth Road in the 1930s.[40]

In 1909 France Hill Estate was sold. A large portion was purchased by the

82   *Tekells Castle after it was damaged by an explosion and fire in 1906.*

France Hill Syndicate, a group of local men including architect Harry Reginald Poulter, sports shop owner James Salter of Aldershot, and estate agent Ferdinand William Baker.[41] Southwell Park Road was built from the Avenue through to Park Street, across what had been part of the grounds of France Hill House. Land to the south of Southwell Park Road, Firwood Road and France Hill Drive was developed by the syndicate. Ferdinand Baker's Dalby Lodge, Far End in France Hill Drive, and Glenwood, Gorse Cottage and The Hovel in Firwood Drive were all designed by Poulter.[42] The remaining estate, the north of Southwell Park Road from The Avenue

83   *Southwell Park Road, looking east. This road was developed after the sale of France Hill Estate in 1909.*

84 *Grand Avenue, formerly the drive to France Hill House, was developed by Alfred Ives.*

85 *The original Over's store, with gas lamps to illuminate the window displays, was situated on Osnaburgh Hill opposite St Michael's Vicarage.*

to Park Street, was acquired by Alfred Ives in March 1910.[43] He developed the old drive to the house, Grand Avenue, and also had the Southern, St Mary and Sinhurst Roads laid out. William Wells King built the fine curved shops and flats on the corner of London Road and Grand Avenue for Ives in 1909 and this set the tone for the type of houses built here.

In town new shops were opening or expanding to serve a growing population, some of which survived through to the late 20th century. Richard Parnell Over established his drapery business in 1857. A single-fronted shop built in 1850 by his father-in-law George Edwards, it was situated on the brow of Osnaburgh hill and for this reason was sometimes known as the Central Store. Initially four of his six sons

86 *A fire destroyed the second Over's store near The Avenue in 1907.*

worked there, but by 1900 only Richard and John remained. It was at this time that a new furniture store was built near The Avenue. This was burnt to the ground in August 1907 and a replacement building, designed by H.R. and B.A. Poulter, took its place.[44]

James Page opened his first shop in High Street in 1904 in a building later converted to the Electric Cinema. He moved to the corner of Obelisk Street and High Street in 1908, formerly Silverthorn Terrace, where the first Council meetings had been held. It was a department store in all senses as the original building had been three terraced dwellings, which meant three sets of stairs led to the upper floors. Page employed a large staff, retaining 28 employees in the First World War.[45] He retired in 1936 when the company name was changed to Page's of Camberley.[46]

Herman Solomon founded his motor business in 1911 in the High Street opposite James Page's store, and from 1914 he was an agent for Ford cars.[47] In 1922 he acquired a house and yard on the corner of St George's Road. This had been James Martin's coal merchants and then Drake & Mount's from 1902, both of whom had cab businesses here in addition to their coal sales.[48] Initially Solomon ran a garage and workshop from here but in 1926 he had a new showroom and workshop erected, capable it is said of having a helicopter land on the roof; it was opened by Admiral Sir Frederick and Lady Tudor.[49] A garage, with petrol pumps that stretched across the pavement, was built in Obelisk Street. Herman Solomon died in June 1935 and the business was managed by his wife Amelia

Established nearly 100 years, and with a wide reputation for all-round service (by which we mean courteous attention, variety in quality goods and utmost value), we are fully equipped to serve YOU . . . . and to serve you well !

R. P. OVER & SONS LTD.

Hire Furnishing Service.

Removals.   Warehousing Baggage.
Agents for the Services.
Housefitting of every description.

Drapers, Milliners, Outfitters, Bootmen, Furniture, Bedding, Carpets, Curtains, China and Glass, Ironmongery

Removals a Speciality.   Distance no object.   Estimates free

87   *The new Over's department store designed by H.R. & B.A. Poulter, with the fleet of trucks outside in the 1930s.*

until his sons Trevor and Gerald were old enough to take it on.

Percy White founded his business in 1907 in London Road, near to the recreation ground.[50] Initially he sold bicycles and sewing machines, but he brought the first petrol pump to the town and from 1919 sold Morris cars. In 1921 he introduced a bus service from Camberley to London. A new petrol station and garage was built on the corner of Knoll Road and London Road in 1928, and by May 1932 the business included a car showroom in the *Cambridge Hotel*, a used car depot in Park Street, a depot and petrol station in Frimley Road and a repair shop in York Road.[51]

JAMES PAGE
.. LADIES' OUTFITTER ..
COSTUMIER & MILLINER

PHONE CAMBERLEY 66
HIGH STREET & OBELISK STREET
CAMBERLEY

88 *James Page's department store on the corner of High Street and Obelisk Street in the 1930s. It was demolished in 1966 and a new building, currently a farmer's market, was erected.*

Jeweller and clockmaker Percy Todd arrived in town at the same time as Percy White, although his name is rarely recalled today. He was well known as a model maker and for training his apprentices. His shop was near the *Cambridge Hotel* and he lived in a small bungalow behind it, which was demolished when Woolworths was built in 1936.[52] He trained the Jack and Hayes brothers, who all became jewellers in town.

He was awarded a silver medal at the Model Engineer Exhibition in 1930 for his working model of a merry-go-round, an accurate replica of the gallopers owned by Whittles fairground. Made from 3,000 tiny pieces, it used to be displayed in his window. After Woolworths was built his son Percy had a shop in Princess Street, where countless small noses would be pressed against the glass to watch the working model.

Six

COLONELSTOWN AND RIBBON DEVELOPMENT

In the 1930s Camberley became known as 'Colonelstown': 'Colonels by the score weave and wobble in and out of traffic on their cycles ... You can't walk in the High Street without bumping into a brace of Brigadiers or spotting a general in a queue.'[1] They could feel quite at home giving their address as Omdurman or Atbara in Gordon Road,[2] or they could dream about their earlier careers in India while living at Ooty or Baroda.[3] Certainly they would not have been short of someone to pass the time of day with as many of the houses in Upper Park Road, Upper Gordon Road and Firwood Drive were occupied by military men and their families. For visitors, the *Duke of York* was an ideal place to stay as the proprietor offered good English fare and comfort, combined with a military atmosphere. Mr Keeling informed potential customers of the hostelry that he was late of the North Staffs Regiment and still a reserve officer.[4]

There was a long tradition of men retiring to Camberley after military service and many of these men had had brilliant careers. There are two VCs buried in St Michael's churchyard and two more at Frimley. Major Thomas Adair Butler was buried at St Michael's Church, Yorktown in May 1901. He lived at Lyndale in Woodlands Road after a career which included being awarded the VC in 1858 for his actions at Lucknow. Colonel Sir Arthur George Hammond was born at Dawlish in 1843 and educated at Sherbourne School. His house in Gordon Road, which was built for him in 1895, was named after his school. He won his VC when a 36-year-old captain serving in the Bengal Staff Corps near Kabul in Afghanistan. He died on 20 April 1919. These men are buried alongside John Whitehead, a Crimean War veteran who lived in Obelisk Street, and Florence Nightingale's batman John Fineghan. At Frimley lies Major-General Charles Mellis, who lived at Five Trees in Tekels Avenue. He retired to Camberley after being awarded his VC at the relief of Kumasi-Ashanti in East Africa in 1900. In 1903 Colonel William George Cubitt, who

89 *A 1920s view from the top of the High Street, with the* Cambridge Hotel *on the left and London County & Westminster Bank on the right. The single-storey buildings on the left were owned by jeweller Percy Todd and sold in 1936 to Woolworth's.*

was in the Indian Army from 1853, was buried at Frimley. He was also awarded his VC at Lucknow in 1857 and lived at Collingwood House in Portsmouth Road.[5] A fifth recipient was Sgt-Major William Lendrum who received his award for bravery at Sebastopol and was buried in the RMC graveyard.

At least eleven Field Marshals attended the RMC and many of these became familiar in the town. Auchinleck attended events at the Royal Albert Orphanage, Haig and Montgomery lived in town, and others were attached to it for various courses over time.[6] Sergeant William Cattermole was awarded a DCM for his part in the Charge of the Light Brigade. He died in 1884 and his grandson Arthur Cattermole

proudly held the medals together with those of his grandfather's relative John Bowen, who was also at the Charge and retired to Camberley.[7] John Capner settled at Yorktown after military service as a 'Private and Faithful servant of Lt-Gen Sir George Scovell serving with him in the campaign of Sir John Moore to Corunna and afterwards the whole of the Peninsula War under the Duke of Wellington'.[8]

In her book about Camberley Ivy Potten recalled a time when shops produced goods specifically for the colleges: 'Saddlers, harness makers and of course tailors of the highest class … there we pawn shops which the cadets frequently u l … second-hand bicycles too were grea vourites … which they threw about wit tter disregard. It

90 *A view from the Yorktown side of Blackwater Bridge towards Camberley with* The Lamb *on the right and the stream and stepping stones over the Wish Stream towards meadowland on the left. This area is barely recognisable today as The Meadows roundabout and newly aligned roads cover most of the land.*

91 *The corner of The Avenue and London Road in the 1920s, with one of the few remaining single-storey cottages built between Yorktown and Cambridge Town.*

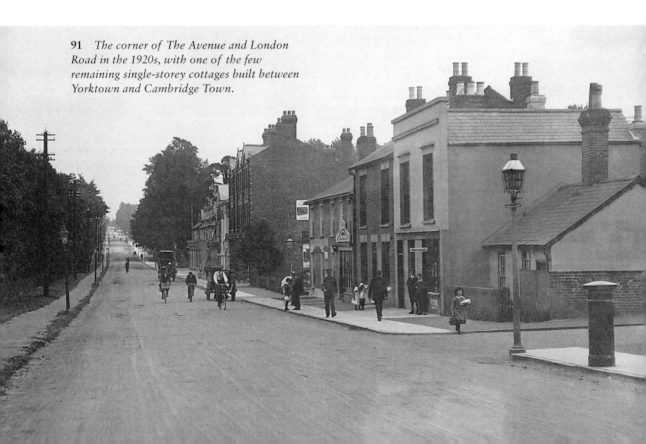

92 *The Avenue with the entrance to Heatherley Road on the right. The road was originally known as Plantation Road as it had been a fir plantation.*

was quite usual to have to walk round an untidy heap of these bikes, with their bars painted in red and white stripes, to match their blazers and round pillbox hats'.[9] Lydia Hart came to Camberley in 1895 and in 1906 founded The Exchange pawn shop in Frimley Road.[10] She became so well-known she was mentioned in music hall skits about the RMC. Wardrobe dealer Arthur Bowdery's shop was in London Road.[11] His son Oliver opened a shop selling second-hand furniture and antiques in Obelisk Street by 1914, a very useful service to those renting property.[12]

During the First World War a great recruitment drive was held, and men were signed up in places including the circus held in 1916 at Doman's meadow. A YMCA canteen opened in the High Street near the recruiting office. Large houses were requisitioned as nursing homes, including Firlands and Heatherbank. It is said the officer class suffered the most casualties. Those listed on the war memorial include

93 *Kings Ride in 1913 seen from the junction with London Road. Many houses here were built by Frank Bath.*

94 *Oliver Bowdery's shop in Obelisk Street dealt in antiques and second-hand furniture.*

Ashton Cadell, the son of Dr Cadell, Edward Davy Pain, son of Arthur Cadlick Pain, the only son of Herbert Hollings of Watchetts, and sons of General Abbot-Anderson, Colonel Boileau, Mr Fowler of Old Dean Hall and Mrs Mackenzie of Collingwood Grange.

Although ex-army personnel predominated in town there were also a number of high-ranking naval men. Vice-Admiral Charles Johnstone lived at Graitney and Admiral Sir Frederick Tudor at Dennistoun. Living at Wargrave in Crawley Ridge was Admiral Sir Frederick Doveton Sturdee, hero of the first battle of the Falklands, who was responsible for preserving the *Victory* at Portsmouth. He is buried at St Peter's, where a piece of wood from the *Victory* forms a cross on his headstone. His burial service was held at St Paul's in 1925. No fewer than

eight Admirals acted as pall-bearers as his coffin processed from St Paul's to St Peter's, and it is said that as the procession reached St Peter's some people were still falling in behind it at St Paul's, almost a mile away.[13] Today he is remembered in the fine stained-glass window at St Paul's.

The water fountain which currently stands near the entrance to the Arena Leisure Centre was erected by public subscription in memory of General Edward Abbot Anderson. Known by local people as 'The General', he had been a student at the RMC, an instructor, and finally a Professor there. After his death in December 1903, £120 was raised and the fountain, built by Adkins the stonemasons, was unveiled exactly one year later. His son Edward did not follow a military career and became better known as the actor Allan Aynesworth.[14]

95 *The interior of St George's Church with its east window dedicated to those who lost their lives in the Boer War.*

RMC, commemorates the death of student Gerald de la Costa Porter, who lost his life in 1882 aboard the *Oxenholme*. One window celebrates the life of Major Francis Taylor, Professor of Military Drawing, who lost his life in the College lake when attempting to save his infant daughter in 1868.[15] St George's Church had a splendid five-light east window, a memorial to those who lost their lives in the Boer War, and a reredos and organ in memory of Major-General Stotherd, who lived at Heathcote House.[16] A memorial on a greater scale altogether was the building of St Tarcisius Church in 1923 to remember all the Catholic men who worshipped here and fell in the Great War. It contains a list of the men,

The town's churches commemorate these military men. At St Michael's the reredos, finely carved by Edward de la Motte of the

96 *The unveiling of the War Memorial by HRH Duke of Connaught in 1922 at the entrance to the Staff College.*

97   *Heather Cottages in Chobham Road, built in 1926 by Frimley Urban District Council.*

many of whom attended services while on courses at the RMC and Staff College, at the north end of the church. It is an almost entirely different list to that on the Cornish granite memorial erected across the

98   *St Tarcisius Church on the corner of London Road and Southern Road was built in 1923 as a memorial to Catholic officers who lost their lives in the First World War.*

road from this church, unveiled by HRH the Duke of Connaught on 30 August 1922 and commemorating all the men from town who lost their lives.[17]

Frimley Urban District Council was keen to provide affordable housing for men returning from service in the First World War. The first social housing, built at Old Dean Road, was ready for occupation in 1921, followed by that in College Ride in 1922. Heather Cottages in Chobham Road were occupied by 1926, and Bristow Road and Frimley Road by 1928.[18] There was also a great expansion in smaller detached and semi-detached housing for the private market. It was a boom time for Frimley Road. It appears local poulterer Nicholas Verran purchased Watchetts estate in 1924 for development rather than his

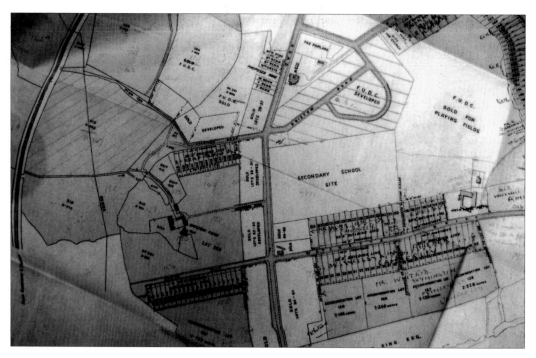

99   *Sale map of 1928 for the Watchetts Estate annotated with the names of local builders who purchased plots.*

own use, and in October 1924 had a new drive laid from Watchetts House to Park Road; known today as Parkway, this had been a narrow carriageway to the house.[19] Verran sold the Council land for Watchetts Recreation Ground in December 1927 and at Crabtree Road for allotments in 1928. In February 1928 he donated the land on which St Mary's Church stands to the parish for the erection of a permanent church. St Mary's, built by William Wells King, was designed by G.G. Lofting and dedicated by the Bishop of Guildford on 22 December 1937.[20] In May 1928 the remaining estate, including 180 acres of land, much of which was farmland stretching from Frimley to Yorktown along the Blackwater River, was auctioned. Land

along Frimley Road, Park Road and Parkway was auctioned in plots of varying size. Watchetts House was purchased by R.P. Over & Sons for £4,200 and 62 plots of land along Frimley Road, Watchetts Drive and Park Road were sold to individual builders for £5,086. These included William Wells King, Ernest Young of Sandhurst, Ray Kemp and George Hoskins. Land nearest Yorktown was purchased by George Doman. The remainder was unsold but was re-auctioned in August 1929. This time the land along Parkway had been divided into smaller plots, most of which were sold to James McLean Keil. Surrey County Council purchased land adjoining Frimley Road, where the Frimley and Camberley Grammar School opened in 1931.

This was a busy period for local builders, a time of ribbon development. Between Watchetts and Yorktown land was developed by the owner of Woodlands and by Mr Harris of the Hollies. Mr Harris employed Ernest Young to build detached houses between his property and Woodlands and in Woodlands Road. Young also built houses in Harcourt Road, Watchetts Drive and the southern end of Frimley Road. In 1931 Reeves Repository was built where the former Woodlands House stood, an essential service in an area where army personnel were moving around.[21] Ray Kemp built houses off Frimley Road, where he had his yard, as well as many fine dwellings in Parkway and Southwell Park Road. Frank Renn had a yard near Crabtree Road, and built houses next to this and in Watchetts.[22]

The offices and workshops of McLean Keil were near the tin church of St Mary's. Known as St Mary's Works, they were surrounded by shops and houses in Krooner Road which he had built in the late 1920s. Housing in Bridge Road was constructed by him in 1937. In part of his yard he built the first factories in 1936, going into partnership with some of the proprietors. With little industry, the depression had marginal impact on the town. Statistics were rarely given but by the end of 1930 the number of unemployed had risen from 138 in March to 427. New factories were welcomed. S. & R. Watts made metal moulding and architectural metalwork, and Aerolex made clips and fastenings. Aerolex's founder Mr Harley was a successful inventor, eventually producing a range of aircraft components.

Headen-Keil Engineering Company, off Victoria Avenue, made gaskets and carburettors for export to Australia, and Rowland Metal Windows in Vale Road made windows, doors and openings.[23] Rowlands was founded by William Rowlands prior to 1929 and was the first industrial unit on the Yorktown estate.[24]

William Wells King had established his yard at Oakley in Frimley Road in 1904. After the First World War he purchased much of the Whins estate from Major Rudge, and had a further yard there from which he was able to extract sand and gravel. He purchased the Donnington estate next to the Whins in the late 1920s. The land was eventually purchased by Lawrence Weaver in 1957 for the development of the Forest Hills estate. Wells King built individual houses or small developments for his workmen or to let to tenants. He also built St Mary's and the Congregational Church in Southwell Park Road.[25] This hexagonal structure, built on land purchased by Nicholas Verran and James Page, was designed by Maurice Lawson and opened for services in October 1930.[26]

Besides Frimley Road, the other area for major development in this period was Kings Ride and College Ride. Almost all the houses built in College Ride and the Diamond Hill area were erected by Farnborough builder Walter Rumble. Ernest Young, George Hoskins and Rumble also built in Old Green Lane. Camberley estate agents Stone and Cowgill purchased land surrounding Diamond Hill house, where they built a range of houses. They advertised them as 'homes amongst

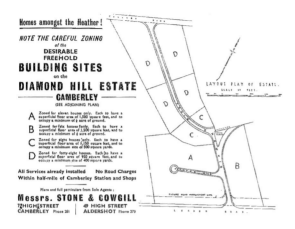

100   *Advertisement for Diamond Hill estate in 1937.*

the heather', and carefully zoned them according to density and size of house.[27]

In the growing town there were more opportunities for private schools. Miss Amy Read left Elmhurst in 1908 when she married local musician Hubert Steele. They lived at Tresillian in France Hill Drive and in 1923 moved to Cheswycks in Firwood Drive, where she opened a pre-preparatory school and he gave music lessons. In the mid-1930s, when they retired to Devon, they sold the school to Mr J. Love.[28] In 1915 Maywood School was owned by Elinor Rimington and by 1920 she had changed the name of the

101   *View from Barossa towards Diamond Hill and College Ride.*

102   *Cordwalles School was also known as Kingswood, Ballard and Wishmore Cross before it became part of the Collingwood complex.*

school and the house to Beaufront. In 1930, after Miss Rimington's death, it was managed by teachers Rosamund Austen and Mary Hele. Miss Austin continued to run the school until the property was requisitioned in the Second World War, the school moving along the road to Mulroy House (formerly Collingwood Towers), which took the name Beaufront, and the old school house, confusingly, reverting to its former name of Maywood.[29] In 1919 Cordwalles, originally established in 1873 at Blackheath, moved in to the Kingswood buildings on London Road, with headmaster the Rev. Mervyn Voules, but at the outbreak of war moved again

to Gloucestershire.[30] In 1919 Miss Herring sold Elmhurst to Miss Crisp and when Foxlease, formerly the home of Dr Nevill Cadell, was put up for sale in 1922 the school moved there, taking the name with them. At this time it was still a general school for kindergarten age children.[31] In the early 1920s Helen Mortimer established the Mortimer School of Dance in the town, and lessons were held in a building behind Stokes Dairy in Park Street.[32] Since most Mortimer pupils attended Elmhurst, Violet Crisp was approached about a dance studio being built within the curtilage of the school. Miss Crisp was of the opinion that dance was not

83

'quite nice',[33] so it took some persuasion, but in 1924 a self-contained studio was erected in the grounds and two years later dance became a major part of the school curriculum. Dance has remained at the heart of the school, with notable young performers including Jenny Agutter and Juliette and Hayley Mills educated there.[34]

Sport regained its popularity and clubs flourished. Watchetts Recreation Ground was officially opened on 16 May 1931 when Frimley Cricket Club invited the chairman of the Council to bowl the first ball. With its additional tennis courts, putting green and pavilion, it became a great asset in town, alleviating the overcrowding at London Road. In 1934 a group of local people including Percy Todd the jeweller established the Blue Pool Company. Land was purchased facing London Road, next to the wooded escarpment on which the Obelisk stands. Work started in February and the pool opened to the public in May 1934.[35] Camberley Football Club moved in 1922 to land off Frimley Road known as Krooner Park, leased from Nicholas Verran, where they still play today. This land was partly paid for with the winnings of a horse named Krooner owned by local estate agent Ferdinand Baker. The first £50 towards the cost was donated after Krooner won a race at Hawthorn Hill in 1922.[36] Admiral Tudor became president of the Camberley Football Supporters Club, formed just after the war, and his wife judged fancy dress, best decorated cycle and the neatest ankle in the Jubilee Fete at Krooner Park in 1935. In August 1932 Thomas King built the stand and changing rooms and

103 *The Blue Pool opened in May 1934.*

these were used for football matches and for the increasingly popular grass track racing held here, which was founded by local councillor Eddie Lawrence.[37]

In November 1929 a new bowling club was formed 'by an amalgamation of the old Camberley (Victoria) Club and the Camberley Recreation Club, a strong, fresh body'.[38] Known as the Camberley Bowls Club, with an HQ at the *Victoria Hotel*, it abandoned the little-used greens at the rear of the hotel. In 1929 the *Camberley News* reported that a cricket club had been formed, which hoped to play games on the recently laid pitch at Watchetts. Local solicitor Mr Close became President and pointed out that when he arrived in Camberley in 1898 he had set up a cricket and hockey club which had run for some years.[39] In 1907 there were two hockey clubs in Camberley, the Pinewood Club, whose secretary was Colonel Pennycuick, and Camberley Club,[40] but it is not clear which one Close had founded. Camberley Commercial Cricket League was established in 1936 and played on Wednesday afternoons. In the first year Solomon's won and runners up were the Yorktown Gas Company employees.[41] Camberley Heath Golf Club flourished and allowed other clubs to use their links, including Heatherside Artisans Club formed in 1932.[42] Molly Gourlay, who was English Golf Champion in the 1920s, became a member of Camberley Heath when she moved to Brackendale Road in 1920[43] and Douglas Bader played there as a guest.[44]

A sport for which Camberley became renowned was motorcycling, and recent histories of the sport regard the town as the place in which it was founded. The first known club was established in 1913, its headquarters at the *Victoria Hotel*. Its first president was Wilfred Styer, a solicitor; captain was Edmund Collins, who owned the Star Mineral Water Works, and chairman was William Hedges, a butcher.[45] The first Southern Scott Scramble was held in 1924. The *Camberley News* reported that

104 *A sketch by G.E. Cox published in the* Camberley News *in 1924 showing the first Southern Scott Scramble.*

'when Camberley and district Motor Club decided to undertake the organisation, it was recognised that they were in for a big thing ... there were in all 89 individual and 18 team entries ... a better course could hardly have been imagined to give the competitors a good sporting test of man and machine'.[46] It included climbing Wild and Woolly on Chobham Ridges, scrambling up High Curley and a steep gradient off Red Road, and is the first known motorcycle scramble race in the country according to enthusiasts.[47] In 1924 those running the club were Percy White, E.J. Over and Harold Cox, architect and captain of the Fire Brigade. The race was won by Arthur Sparks of Fleet, a member of the Camberley Club who opened a garage near the *Jolly Farmer* which is still there today. Another first for Camberley was a Moto-ball, or motorcycle football match,

played between clubs from Middlesbrough and Camberley in 1923.

There were also a number of new societies and clubs. The Choral and Orchestral Society was founded by Hubert and Amy Steele in 1921. Hubert was organist at St Paul's and St George's and made a living by offering musical tuition. Rehearsals were held at the Wesleyan Church Hall, with performances at the Drill Hall. Members of Dr Twort's family, all of whom played musical instruments, were joined by a choir consisting of over fifty men and women.[48] In October 1932 Steele resigned as conductor over the difficulty of obtaining male voices.[49] It was a difficult time for musical societies. The Operatic Society was founded by conductor Mr Spyer in 1927, who reached deadlock over the use of the Drill Hall in 1932 when work became necessary before a licence for

105 *Sparks Garage near the* Jolly Farmer *in the 1950s.*

performances could be given. At the same time the Camberley Music Society, also run by Hubert Steele, closed down.[50]

Lack of suitable accommodation for societies was partly alleviated when the Agincourt Hall opened for business. The new hall, built on to the side of Agincourt House, opened in November 1929.[51] The old house was converted, with a Masonic Hall at its heart designed by H.R. Poulter for the Albert Edward Lodge. The Agincourt Hall Company was established to run the venue with Percy White as its secretary. It opened with a review, and by January 1931 visitors could also enjoy an indoor 'midget' 18-hole golf course.[52]

The Arcade cinema owned jointly by George Doman and his son-in-law Ray Fairs was officially opened in 1923 by Major-General Sir Edmund Ironside. It was named after the arcade of shops lining its entrance, which included Minnie Clare's hat shop and Saunders wool and toy shop. The Regal, later known as the Odeon, Classic and latterly Robins, opened in August 1932. The Electric Cinema in the High Street closed in 1926 when plans to erect a new building at the rear of the *Cambridge Hotel* fell through and the old building was adapted for use as Robert's furniture store. The Academy at Yorktown closed in 1929 and was converted for use as a furniture repository.[53]

A relay radio system was set up in July 1932 when a London firm applied to erect a wireless receiver and connect it to a central distributing exchange at Relay House in Southwell Park Road. Each

106   *Advert for Relay Radio in 1937.*

subscriber was connected to the receiver by wires over streets in the district. A speaker was installed in each house and users paid a small sum each week for the service.[54] Television was first shown in Rosedeane in Gordon Road in 1928, at the home of Mr Alford,[55] but televisions did not go on sale in town until 1937. Council members watched the first demonstration

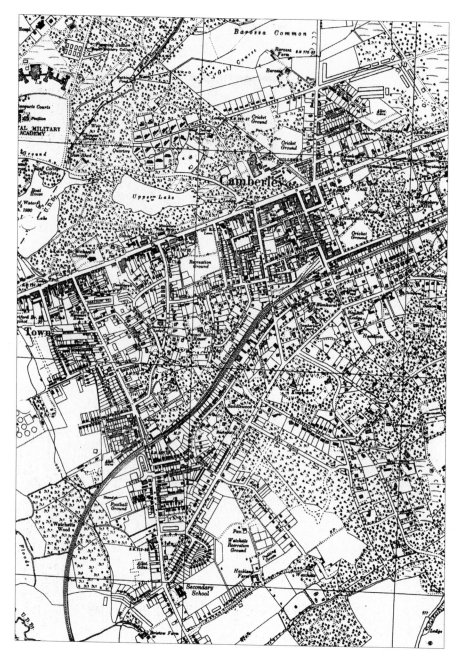

107 The 1938 OS map of Camberley.

at Camberley Radio Supplies. Camberley was outside the range of Alexandra Palace receptivity and a decent picture was only possible in houses situated on high ground around the town.[56]

A short-lived attraction, closed by the outbreak of the Second World War, was the Surrey Border and Camberley Railway. Established to provide a longer route than the earlier Foxhill Miniature Railway, it

108 Surrey Border & Camberley Railway advertisement December 1938, using a photograph taken when Graham Moffatt launched the railway in July of that year.

ONE HUNDRED ARRIVE — ONE HUNDRED DEPART

PICTURESQUE SCENERY
A MARVEL OF ENGINEERING ACHIEVEMENT
Come and Test the Power of Steam

SPECIAL CHEAP EXCURSIONS
from 5.30 p.m. on SUNDAYS
ALL THE WAY 1/- **RETURN**

FARNBOROUGH GREEN STATION,   CAMBERLEY STATION,
FARNBOROUGH, Hants.   CAMBERLEY, Surrey.

carried passengers from Frimley Bridge to Moorlands Road. Opened on 23 July 1938 by actor Graham Moffatt, it was the brainchild of engineer H.C. Bullock and A. Kinloch, a merchant banker. Surrey and Border Avenue (now Avenue Sucy) was named after it.[57] The electrification of the main railway through town took place just prior to the outbreak of war in 1939 and gave the workers at Solomon's garage the ideal theme for their Camberley Carnival entry, providing a little fun before the bleakness of the war years.[58]

109 Solomon's Camberley Carnival entry in 1939 celebrated the electrification of the line through Camberley.

Seven

The Second World War and After

During 1938 and 1939 preparations were made for the outbreak of war. In September 1938 fitting of gas masks took place at St Mary's, St George's and St Paul's church halls, and each person took a respirator home with them. Trenches for bomb shelters were dug at recreation grounds, Victoria Avenue and Knoll Road, and residents were encouraged to provide their own. A trial blackout was observed from 9.30 to 10.30p.m. on 28 September 1938 when all street lights were extinguished, windows and doors covered and motorists instructed to turn off headlights.[1] By the time war was declared air-raid posts had been established, first-aid posts set up at The Poplars and Frimley Hospital and cleansing centres at London Road and Watchetts recreation grounds.[2] Evacuees arrived, 200 mothers in the first wave, accompanied by 150 children under school age.[3] France Hill House was requisitioned for evacuees from Croydon, and Fir Trees in Norwich Avenue and Beechleigh in Brackendale Road were used for schools from London. Corinna in

The Avenue became a nursery school for evacuees[4] and another was set up at the old *Criterion* pub in Yorktown in 1943. Local schoolchildren joined the war effort, Lyndhurst pupils supplying troops with 10,000 cigarettes[5] and Elmhurst children entertaining evacuees.[6] In 1941, following the Nazi invasion of the Channel Islands, daughters of the Dame of Sark arrived and were housed in Bath Road.[7] Towards the end of the war evacuees arrived from Bognor Regis, and Pinehurst in Park Road was requisitioned to house them.[8] In 1945 there were still 200 evacuees in Camberley, including an elderly Russian man, and they were joined in July 1945 by Dutch children sent over for short holidays.[9] Requisitioned properties included The Knoll for the Royal Engineers, Hillside for the Air Ministry, where it is said Forest Yeo-Thomas, better known as SOE agent 'White Rabbit' was stationed, and Cordwalles School and Beaufront for the Auxiliary Training Service. The ATS used the grounds of Cordwalles for training young women to drive and make repairs to their vehicles. One member of the ATS in 1944 was Princess Elizabeth, who arrived each day to join her group at Beaufront and famously had her mother, Queen Elizabeth, visit her at Cordwalles.[10]

The RMC and Staff College became known as OCTU, Officer Cadet Training Unit, and men were brought here for short courses before being sent abroad. Alexander Ralli of Frimley Park became the first individual to purchase a Spitfire for the RAF in 1940, and the main wings of his home were used to house a maternity unit, where over 1,000 babies were born, and a convalescent home for officers for the duration.[11] A further convalescent home was established at Old Dean Hall in Crawley Ridge in 1941.[12] Camberley residents purchased their own Spitfire in 1941,[13] as well as raising over £120,000 in five days for War Weapons Week. The following year over £75,000 was raised to provide two tanks named *Frimley* and *Camberley*,[14] and £144,000 raised in Warship Week went towards adopting HMS *Vestal*.[15]

The war brought factories and workers to the area, escaping the expected bombing in London. Existing works were expanded and a concrete pipe works, known as Bates, which had opened in the spring of 1925 in London Road, was taken over by Eastwoods in December 1937.[16] McLean Keil, a First World War pilot, built more factories on his land as war approached, with access from Krooner Road and Bridge Road.[17] These factories included Linatex, founded in Bermondsey in 1926 by Bernard Wilkinson, a young British rubber planter. While working in Malaya he had experimented with a unique process of

110 *During the Second World War the military colleges became known as OCTU, Officer Cadet Training Centre. These huts were set up in the grounds of the RMC to house the large numbers of men passing through the system.*

cold vulcanization. The company moved to Camberley in 1939, where it made self-sealing protective coating for fuel tanks and metal fuel pipes. It was also involved in manufacturing the Pluto pipeline which pumped fuel across the Channel after D Day.[18] Aerolex moved into one of Keil's new factories, where it made a range of harnesses and belts for stowing items in aircraft, as well as aeroplane parts. In the 1950s the factory employed 200 people making items similar to those produced during the war.[19] Another newcomer, British Gas & Torch, distributed propane under the trade name of Torchgas and made torches and nozzles, including those suitable for under-water use. The factory was doubled in size in 1942 and operated night as well as day shifts. The factory doubled in size

again after the war and took on extra staff, almost all of whom were women. Vivian Loyd was established in January 1940 by Sir John Carden, who lived at Carwarden House, and Captain Loyd of Copped Hall. They manufactured small tanks used as bren-gun and personnel carriers. At the end of hostilities they produced a tractor based on the design of the tanks. Known as the Loyd Crawler Tractor, it was especially useful in difficult farming conditions.[20]

Schools remained open during holidays so that mothers could continue to work in the factories. Unless they had children under school age, they were required to participate in some form of voluntary services. Some joined the AFS, the precursor to the National Fire Service, and a factory fire service was set up by Aerolex

111 *The interior of Aerolex, which made belts and harness for stowing equipment in aircraft, in the Second World War.*

and Linatex. Others provided medical aid. The Surrey 14 and 18 Red Cross Units were housed at The Poplars in Frimley Road, with Dr Twort and Sister Tringham in charge.[21] The Commandant of Unit 14 was Dorothy Worsley, whose father Canon St John Brodrick had been Chaplain to Queen Victoria. She had been the first female Chairman of the Council (1935-8) and had a wartime fire engine named *Dorothy* after her.[22] Other women took up fire-watching, became wardens or made refreshments for troops. Three ladies refused to play any part in the effort, and were imprisoned rather than join fire-fighters or pay a £5 fine. The Misses Dungay were pacifists and members of the Theosophist Church at Tekels Park, and owned a vegetarian restaurant in Frimley Road known as Deborah's.[23]

112 *Carden Loyd tractors were made utilising equipment and designs first used to make tanks in the Second World War.*

Parkland was used for growing crops, including wheat and potatoes on the rugby field and bowling greens at Watchetts,[24] although people were encouraged to use the remaining parkland. The Holiday at

113 *Members of the Factory Fire Service. Ida and Joan Croombs are on the left.*

93

114 *The Red Cross Unit at the Poplars in Frimley Road.*

Home scheme, an attempt to stop people from travelling, was popular. Sports, teas, Punch and Judy, and the arrival of the funfair or circus brought fun to town and records were purchased by the Council so that open-air dancing could be held.[25] In wet weather shows were held at Caird Hall and Camberley Working Men's Club.[26]

A tented camp was hastily erected on Old Dean Common for men returning from Dunkirk, and following the fall of France this was taken over by the Free French forces. Nissen huts were erected to house them and the Canadian and New Zealand troops. De Gaulle was a frequent visitor to Camberley, staying on at least one occasion at Mossy Croft (now White Oaks) in Southwell Park Road.[27] The Free French, who used Blackbushe Airport for missions to France, left Camberley in June 1945. The camp

was occupied by German prisoners of war until the late 1940s when facilities included a small chapel; when this closed a wooden cross made by the prisoners was presented to St Michael's Church.[28]

Air-raid warning sirens were placed on top of the Council Offices and at Yorktown gasworks. In 1942 local residents requested that the Relay Radio service be used to sound the Alert and All Clear, and this was agreed. It is believed German bombers were looking for the RMC and Staff College lakes, and as these had been drained they mistakenly bombed Watchetts lake area. Langlands and Marlow, two houses opposite the Grammar School, were demolished after a raid on 19 March 1941.[29] Sarah Marlow died of a heart attack brought on by the shock of discovering her home, Langlands, had been destroyed, but she was the only local person to die. One raid did hit the College stables and a house in the RMC Terrace was lost. In October and November 1940 property was damaged at Old Green Lane, Watchetts Drive, Waverley Drive, Church Hill, Upper Park Road, Knightsbridge Road and Tekels Park. All local builders were involved in the scheme to repair houses and build shelters, warden posts and water storage tanks. Some travelled to London to repair properties.

VE Day was marked by two days of celebrations in London Road Recreation Ground. The park was floodlit and dancing continued into the evenings. Local staff

were given the day off work and sports and teas were provided for all.[30]

In 1947 the RMC became the Royal Military Academy, an amalgamation of the RMA at Woolwich and the RMC at Sandhurst. The following year Barossa Common was the site for Olympic equestrian events, accommodation for the riders and their mounts being provided within the College grounds. The Olympic torch took a route along the Guildford Road, through Bisley and Lightwater and then through Bagshot Park, on its way to Wembley. The games provided much interest and colour during an otherwise

115 _Platoon 5 of C Company of the 1st Surrey Home Guard photographed at the front of the Aerolex factory in Bridge Road._

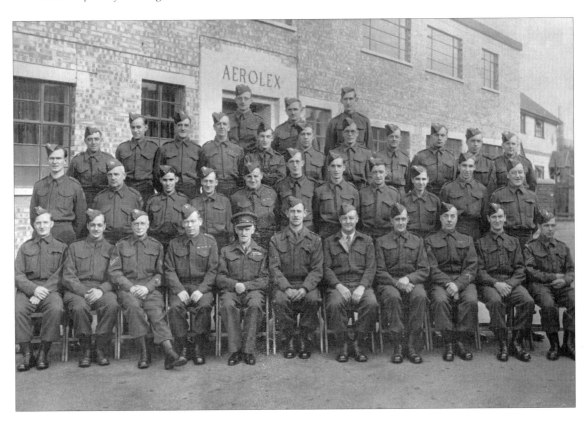

116 *Residents of Bristow Road and Crescent celebrating the Coronation at the Watchetts Recreation Ground Pavilion in 1953.*

drab time.[31] The Coronation in 1953 provided the town with another excuse to deck their houses and organise street parties.

Large houses, now too expensive to maintain, were converted to flats to ease the housing situation and prefabs were erected in Surrey and Border Avenue. Athallan Grange was purchased by the Rheostatic Company, rooms in the old mansion becoming workshops, and The Poplars became a local clinic following the establishment of the National Health Service. Frimley Hall, which had been converted to a hotel in 1935, was purchased by Peter Shepherd in 1949. His wife ran a riding school in the grounds and by 1953 Peter had established a mink farm.[32] David Shepherd, his son, was living in London at the time, working at a studio in Chelsea, where his tutor was marine artist Robin Goodwin. He had painted scenes of London, hoping to sell them to those attending the Coronation; now he is well known for his depictions of wildlife and as a conservationist.[33]

Expansion of the area was the burning local issue. A proposal to transfer families from Metropolitan Surrey to Camberley was initiated by the Minister of Housing in December 1949.[34] The plan involved moving 10,000 people, building homes, new schools, churches and a new town centre, and providing employment for them in factories with key-worker housing. In 1953 a firm commitment to the scheme remained, but it was reduced in scale to 6,000 people. Camberley would not be a 'new town' as much of the land suitable for expansion was owned by the War Office and, at a time when the Cold War was an issue, they were unwilling to release it.[35]

117   *The production line at Southern Instruments photographed by Ron Francis in 1962.*

In addition to the factories opened during the war, new industrial estates were planned at Yorktown and the Frimley end of Frimley Road. Most small firms setting up in Camberley and Frimley supplied the new electronics industry. Aeronautical Radio Services Ltd was the first company to move in to Doman Road in 1954. They were contractors to the Admiralty and Ministry of Aviation and renowned for the production of electronic and ancillary equipment, especially radar and transceivers. Southern Instruments moved to their new factory in Frimley Road. They made a wide range of goods, including oscillograph recording equipment. Ansafone was a subsidiary of Southern Instruments, which was also later known by the name of Storno or Storno Southern. They made telephone answering machines and are believed to have been the only manufacturer producing this type of electronic recording equipment in the country. They also introduced the first recording machines to be used inside a vehicle and on motorbikes.[36] Ancillary Developments was founded in 1946 by local businessmen Percy White and McLean Keil. Originally based at Blackbushe Airport and in the Frimley Road, it moved to a new factory unit in Surrey Avenue in 1956. Ancillary designed and produced camera equipment for RAF target aircraft and other scientific instruments. In 1964 it

118   *Joyce Chuter and her manager photographed at the door of the Yorktown branch of John Farmer in 1949.*

97

119 *London Road, Camberley, with the old Arcade Cinema on the left and Post Office beyond it, photographed in the 1950s. The Arcade became Red Cottage Gardens nursery.*

doubled its workforce to meet demand for one of its developments, the potentiometer, an electronic device designed to keep aircraft and missiles on course.

Better known names moving to town were Janitor Boilers, All Wheel Drive and Unibond. Janitor Boilers was established in Vale Road, Camberley by 1951, and made solid fuel boilers for the domestic market. In the early 1960s they were known as Powell Duffryn and by 1967 as International Janitor. All Wheel Drive was founded by Bill Andrews in Ascot and moved in to Yorktown in 1955, initially employing just 22 people. The workforce had increased to almost 700 by 1961. In 1958 the company was licensed to produce and market Michigan construction machinery and in 1961 it purchased the old US Navy hangar at Blackbushe to enable them to boost their exports. From December 1964 it traded under the name of Clark Equipment. A further 700 people were employed and the company won the Queens Award for exports in 1966.[37] Unibond was founded in Camberley in 1953 under the name of Liquitile Supply & Surfex Flooring by father and son Malcolm and Raymond Busby. They had an office in the High Street and a small production works in a converted stable in the goods yard at Camberley Station. Initially they produced a range of powder and liquid floor finishes. In 1958 Raymond took over the business and in 1962 moved into

120 *Park Street Post Office and general store in the 1950s when owned by the Alborough family. It closed in 1985.*

a factory in Glebeland Road. In the early 1970s this was replaced by a larger factory in Tuscam Way.[38].

After employment, housing was the greatest post-war need. Old Dean, the largest social housing estate in Camberley, was planned initially for local people. Shortage of materials led the Council to decide on a mix of house types, Cornish timber-framed, concrete slabs, steel-framed houses with a brick exterior and wood-wool internal slabs, and conventional brick housing. It was the brick housing that, despite the pre-fabricated nature of the alternatives, was finished first and at the cheapest price. The first house was ready for occupation in September 1953. In December 1955 a further 80 acres was purchased from the War Office for building houses for Metropolitan families, and in June 1956 representatives of Wimbledon Borough Council came to town to view the facilities. A bus took them on a tour of the Old Dean, followed by other sites chosen for their homes, next to Heather Cottages in Chobham Road, at Rorkes Drift in Mytchett, and James Road. They also looked at a new school in the course of erection and at Yorktown Industrial Estate.[39]

By August 1964 the first phase of 1,177 houses at Old Dean was ready and further land was purchased. There were new shops, garage and recreation grounds, and a public house, *The Highwayman*, built by Spear & King, opened in September 1961. This became locally famous for the jazz sessions held here, including a televised BBC broadcast and an appearance by Dudley Moore in January 1966.[40] Road names were associated with the history of

the area. Caesar's Camp was named after the nearby Iron-Age hill fort, Star Post and Saddleback were features on local maps, and Lorraine Road and School were named after the Free French Camp. Later names recalled where the new townsfolk had come from: Sutton, Wallington, Mitcham, Wimbledon, Esher and Surbiton. St Peter and St Paul Catholic Church, built by Spear & King using a 17th-century barn at its central core, was consecrated by the Bishop of Southwark in June 1963.[41] St George's in Knoll Road closed in 1966

121   The Highwayman *public house on the Old Dean Estate, photographed by Ron Francis. It opened in 1961, closed in 1988, and was demolished in 1990.*

122   *St Peter and St Paul Catholic Church was built with a 17th-century barn at its heart. Here the original barn frame has been erected prior to the modern outer shell being built over it*

123 *St Martin's Church is named after the 4th-century Bishop of Tours, a link with the Free French troops stationed near here in the war.*

and the fine five-lancet east window was selected to go to the new stained glass museum at Ely, but was demolished along with the church in 1973.[42] St Martin's was consecrated in January 1978 by the Bishop of Dorking. Money raised by selling land on which St George's had stood was put towards St Martin's, the remainder being found through fundraising. When completed, just £4,000 of the total cost of £90,000 was outstanding. The church was named after the fourth-century Bishop of Tours, providing a further link with the Free French.[43]

An essential facility for the growing community was a larger hospital. In June 1957 it was proposed that Frimley Park house would be converted for this use, an extension of its wartime role as a maternity unit and convalescent home.[44] The Council anticipated a population of 40,000 by 1970, which was a good estimate as it stood at 44,965 in 1971,[45] but it was not until January 1964 that a decision was made to build a new hospital on land to the rear of Frimley Park.[46] In 1958 Frimley and Camberley Urban District Council had adopted a plan which involved moving residents, schools and a small car park from the centre of Camberley and building a new shopping centre. At a public meeting held at the

124 *Mark Bonham-Carter digging the first sod of land on the site of Frimley Park Hospital, which took its name from Frimley Park House. The hospital was built on land formerly attached to the house. It opened in September 1974.*

Agincourt on 18 May 1960 the estimated cost of the scheme was given as between £2 and 4,000,000. There were, however, obstacles in the way. These included the compulsory purchase of houses, many now owned by landlords who had seen the possibility for development, and Surrey County Council, who owned Camberley School and were unwilling to release the site until 1970.[47] The school briefly became the focus of media attention when pupil Hugh Edwards won the role of Piggy in the 1963 film *The Lord of the Flies*, a dramatization of Golding's book in which Piggy tells the 'littluns' about the history of Camberley!

In August 1962 drawings were submitted for a new store for Harvey's of Guildford on the corner of Park Street and Princess Street,[48] and in October of that year it was estimated that the cost of rehousing the 260 families still living in town would be £1,000,000. In February 1964 the first £100,000 was spent on compulsory purchase deals, and by March 1965 almost all properties had been acquired, costing the Council over £744,000.[49] Arndale Property Trust agreed in principal to develop the site in partnership with the Council in 1965, the deal being finalised on 14 June 1966. The proposed design included 104 shops,

125   *Eight pairs of twins were photographed in the playground of Camberley School just prior to its closing. The building in the background was the Infant School.*

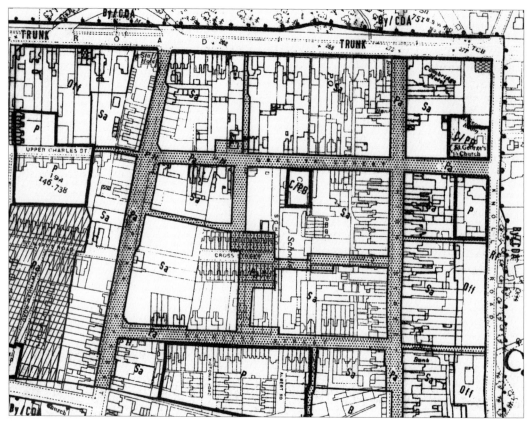

126 *Map of the proposed changes to the town centre in 1964. The original street plan has been overlaid with the new shopping centre.*

with maisonettes and flats above those in Obelisk Street and Grace Reynolds Walk, and an open space in the centre to be known as Town Square. The plans were approved by the government in December 1966 and building work commenced rapidly to avoid the Development Levy due to come into force in April 1967. It took until April 1972 for the scheme to be realised and for shopkeepers to move in, and it was June before the centre was fully open.[50] Sainsburys, Boots and MacFisheries moved from the High Street and the Co-operative store from its former site next to the Council Offices in London Road. Tesco, Superdrug, Halfords

and other national retailers arrived along with smaller privately owned businesses, including Chapman's shoes and Camberley Travel. Seating areas, trees and shrubs and a water-feature at the rear of Harvey's were all provided, but none of the plants lasted long and the water feature was taken out almost immediately because of vandalism.

Schools were another priority. On 3 July 1947 France Hill Secondary School was officially opened by Harold Watkinson MP at France Hill House, with William Steel, a former teacher at Yorktown School, as its head.[51] Lorraine opened on Old Dean Estate in 1957 and in 1958 a new France

Hill School was built in Watchetts Drive, although initially all but the top classes remained at France Hill Drive. In 1960 St Tarcisius moved from Obelisk Street to The Knoll and Cordwalles Infant School and Bristow Primary on James Road estate opened in 1961. In 1964 Barossa Secondary School was built adjoining the old Ballard School, and in 1968 Frimley and Camberley Grammar School moved to new premises within sight of both of them. These were amalgamated in 1971 when the school became known as Collingwood. Wishmore Cross was a residential school for special needs pupils which opened at Ballard in 1960, and when it moved to

Chobham in 1972 the buildings were used by Collingwood's sixth-form pupils.[52]

There were a growing number of private schools. In 1953 Little Folks School in Upper Park Road, a nursery and preparatory school with daily boarders, and St Monica's at Crawley Ridge, for children up to 12 years old, were both using the Montessori method of teaching, St Monica's offering to collect pupils from Lightwater, Bagshot, Windlesham and Frimley.[53] Gay Trees was a kindergarten in Grand Avenue run by Ivy Potten, who also entertained children by offering Punch and Judy sessions. In 1960 Cheswycks moved from Firwood Drive to purpose-built premises at Frimley

127 *An aerial view of the town centre in 1970, looking east towards the library and Civic Hall. Camberley School has been demolished and the steel structure of the new shops is rising in its place.*

TOWN CENTRE

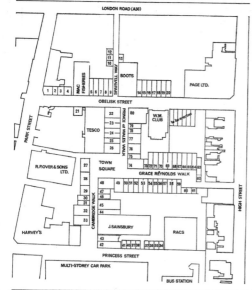

128 *The town centre layout in 1973.*

service since the early days of the furniture store, when goods were transported by horse pantechnicon, and this was the only part of the business to carry the name into the 21st century.[55] In 1961 Page's planned a new building with rooftop parking, and a lift in Obelisk Street which would convey cars to the roof. This came to nothing, but plans drawn up in April 1964 were acted on. Now part of the United Drapery Stores Group, their old premises were demolished in January 1966 and a new store built by Spear & King.[56] Completion of the last phase of work took place in April 1967, and the opening coincided with the 63rd anniversary of the company's founding. In 1979 the name was changed from Pages to Allders and Pete Murray and Monty Modlyn relaunched it, driving around town in a vintage car led by the band of the R.M.A.[57]

New factories offered sports and leisure facilities and additional clubs were formed in town. Hillside was acquired from the Air Ministry by the Council in June 1960 as part of the general acquisition of property for the Civic Building Development Scheme in Knoll Road, and rooms were let to a growing number of societies, including Frimley and Camberley Society of Arts, Camberley Pictorialists and Camberley Players. Spartan Boys' Club used Hillside Coach House.[58] In April 1962 this was the proposed site for a new police station, and in December 1966 the building was sold to Surrey County Council for that purpose, land behind being used to build Portesbery School and Hillside residential unit for adults with special needs. Camberley Natural History Society was founded in 1947, with Maxwell Knight as its chairman.[59] Major Maxwell Knight

Green, and eventually amalgamated with Clewborough House School which had opened in 1969. The old Camberley School situated at the heart of all development was demolished and re-housed at France Hill in 1968, eventually occupying a purpose-built school in the grounds.[54]

Over's continued trading in both London Road shops until March 1965 when it moved to a new store in Park Street (currently Primark). They had provided a removals had lived at Ropley House in London Road for much of the war and was an expert in counter-subversion for MI5. Many believe that 'M', in the James Bond novels, is based on Knight, Fleming's colleague in the Department of Naval Intelligence. After the war Knight lived in Camberley and became widely known as a broadcaster and writer on natural history topics.[60] George Lodge, another member of the Natural History Society, was an artist and taxidermist living at Hawk House in Upper Park Road. He numbered amongst his notable visitors Lord Alanbrooke, who wrote the Foreword to Lodge's *Birds of the British Isles*. His mounted specimens form the basis of the collection at Surrey Heath Museum.[61] The Windlesham Camera Club, which changed its name to Windlesham and Camberley Camera Club in 1950, had been founded by John Hayward in 1935. In 1948 their Patron was Princess Elizabeth, who lived at Windlesham Moor after her marriage to Prince Phillip. In 1949 she opened their exhibition at the Working Men's Club and invited committee members to her home to take photographs.[62] The Natural History and Camera Clubs are two of the societies still thriving in town.

Camberley Carnival was held each year, floats representing most of the local societies and businesses. Visiting circuses arrived by train and the elephants would amble, trunk attached to tail of animal in front, along the High Street and London Road to the Recreation Ground, where the big top was set up. Father Christmas also arrived by train, a sleigh waiting to transport him to Page's store. Since the early 20th century, when there had been

129 *Grace Reynolds Walk photographed by David Howells in 1985, when there were a number of small individual shops including butchers and greengrocers.*

130 *Billy Smart's Circus elephants arrived in town by train. They are seen leaving the railway station before being led up the High Street in 1952.*

church football teams, there had been no youth teams in town. A group of newspaper delivery boys, most of whom were Grammar School pupils, were encouraged to form a team by their employer Bill Weston, whose shop was in Obelisk Street; they called it Camberley Wanderers. Formed in the 1948-9 season, they cycled to matches in Broadmoor, Sandhurst, Cove and Mytchett. They joined the Ascot Minor League and were featured on Tony East's Under-20 Parade Show on BBC Radio.

131 *Camberley Wanderers youth football team in 1949.*

Among the players were Bob and Ron Tindall. Ron, a magnificent all-rounder, played football for Chelsea and West Ham, and cricket for Surrey. In 1967 the team merged with Camberley Football Club.[63]

It was not until 1946, when men returned from the war, that the modern Camberley Cricket Club was established, initially playing on a pitch at the Staff College. In 1947 seven acres of land off Parkway was offered to them. Bert Lock, head groundsman at The Oval, inspected the site and made suggestions for its treatment. Mr Crook of Park Farm ploughed and harrowed it and planted potatoes as a cleansing crop, while members picked stones and filled in the wartime tank-traps. It was officially opened in 1952.[64] Those who have played for the club include Tony Lock and Shaun Udal, the current

President, who played for county teams and England. He started playing for the club in 1984, his father Robin celebrating 35 years with them in 1987. One of the most notable female cricketers of her generation lived at Myrtlewood in Heathcote Road. Myrtle Maclagan played in the first women's test team to tour Australia in 1934-5. In 1937 she scored a century against Australia at Blackpool and took all ten wickets in one match. Appointed an MBE in 1966, she died in 1993.[65] Local boys continued to enjoy scrambling on local heathland, but there were those who took to the newer scooters. In 1956 seven enthusiastic Lambretta owners founded the Lucky Seven Scooter Club in Camberley. In 1958, when it held the Lambretta Club National Rally at London Road Recreation Ground, it had 800 members.[66]

--- Eight ---

THE MODERN TOWN

'Camberley' Kate could always be heard before being seen as she was accompanied by the barking of dogs piled into or attached by lead to her cart. Kate Ward was born in Middlesbrough in 1895 and came to Camberley to work at the RMC. She lived in a terraced house next to *The Lamb* at Yorktown. At the wedding of Princess Elizabeth she sent a dog lead as a present, an indication, perhaps, of what lay in store. She first rescued a dog in 1943 and by the 1960s regularly looked after thirty of them.[1] They all lived in the rear ground-floor room of her small terraced cottage. Not all the dogs were strays as she took in paying boarders and raised money for dog food by allowing her photograph to be taken. She became more widely known after a film of her walking her dogs on Barossa Common was made by Lord Snowdon in October 1968.[2] Felicity Edwards, a descendant of naturalist and author Richard Jeffries, lived in Frimley Road. She had nine cats, two dogs and Nelly the hen. Her Persian cat had been

rescued on VJ night after being doused in petrol and set alight. All her animals were given amazing names, a cat with no teeth being known as Mrs Honoria Bracegirdle, and the long-haired dachshunds as Victoria Hilltrees and Shadrach.[3]

These ladies and their pets are not the only things linking Camberley to a strange assortment of wildlife. In 1944 a gentleman purchasing a house in town thought there might be something wrong with his roof. Mr Warren, the Council Sanitary Inspector, found evidence of the house longhorn beetle, or 'Camberley Beetle' as it became known. It infests roof timbers, eating through the inside of the strut while the outer edges appear normal. Only two isolated cases had been notified in England since the 1880s, but when 'a team of experts picked houses and business premises at random throughout the district ... [it] found that at least 520 acres of Camberley was under attack'.[4] The government sent an entomologist to study the beetle, about which little was known, and after intensive research a solution was found. Houses in the area still have to have their roof timbers specially treated. The beetle, which is usually found in Scandinavia, is thought to have arrived in town either from a travelling trunk stored in a loft from where the beetle was able to migrate to roof timbers, or by the importation of timber from Scandinavia.

In October 1969 Camberley became the only place in Britain in almost fifty years to have a full-scale action plan put in place because of a rabid dog. Fritz, a two-year old terrier owned by Major Hemsley of Kings Ride, showed symptoms of the disease and attacked people in the vicinity of the house. The dog had been in quarantine in Folkestone, but rabies was later detected in another dog held there. Fritz had attacked one of Stokes dairymen, whose skin had not been punctured, but he and several children had been licked by the dog, including Major Hemsley's sons and daughter, and all were vaccinated. In all, 27 people were treated and one hospitalised as a result. All wildlife in the grounds of the colleges and

132 'Camberley Kate' with her cart full of dogs photographed in October 1968, when a film was made about her. Lord Snowdon is on the extreme left carrying a megaphone and Desmond Wilcox, the husband of Esther Rantzen, appears to be trying to organise the dogs.

133   *All wildlife in the Kings Ride area was culled in October 1969, after a rabid dog was exercised on common land here. In this photograph, taken by* Camberley News *photographer Mike Hawley, the men are setting off to kill foxes, badgers, squirrels and any other animals likely to carry the virus.*

at Barossa and Old Dean Commons were culled, and no dogs were exercised without muzzles.[5] It was July 1970 before dogs could be exercised locally without one.[6]

A concrete elephant stands opposite Homebase in London Road, Yorktown, formerly Eastwoods. The factory was owned by Trollope & Colls in the 1960s and in 1963 they invited artist and writer Barbara Jones to design a model from their concrete pipes which could be towed through London as part of the Lord Mayor's Show. All but the ears were made from their standard pipes.[7] In June 1964 the company were granted permission to stand the elephant at the entrance to their

134   *Trollope & Colls concrete elephant photographed by Ron Francis in 1965, when it stood at the entrance to their yard at Yorktown.*

yard.[8] In 1982 part of the trunk fell off and in November 1987 it was painted all over with large black spots,[9] but despite these mishaps and an occasional graffiti attack the elephant is now a locally listed structure.

Camberley in the 1950s and 1960s had its own cultural life, with thriving arts and music societies. The High Curley Stompers

135   *A Christmas card sent by Chas McDevitt to his friends in the 1950s. He is photographed with Shirley Douglas, who became his wife.*

136   *Camberley High Street, looking south with Pages on the right, after a heavy fall of snow in January 1963.*

were established in 1951 by Peter Honri, who lived at Dunross Farm in Lightwater and was a full-time entertainer, appearing in films and television programmes. Camberley's Chas McDevitt, Neil Manders and Marc Sharratt became members of the group, which played regularly at the *Victoria Hotel* in the early 1950s, and at other venues around the south of England. Chas, who lived at Uplands Road, eventually led the group and became a household name in 1957 when, partnered by Nancy Whiskey, he released the hit single 'Freight Train'. It was also a hit in America, where the duo toured and appeared on the Ed Sullivan Show. Chas opened the Soho Freight Train Café, which became a magnet for skiffle group members, including Tommy Steele.[10] Also living in Uplands Road was singer Julian Lee, also known as Julian X, whose recording of 'I Can't Wait' was released in 1960. In the 1960s Yvonne and Heather Wheetman became well-known backing group Su and Sunny. They made a debut recording in 1963 as The Myrtelles, became part of the Stockingtops group, and released ten records between 1965 and 1972 as Su and Sunny. In 1969 they formed the backing group for Joe Cocker on his album *A Little Help from my Friends*.[11]

Café society came to Camberley, young people sipping frothy coffee while listening to a juke box. In the 1950s they could choose from the Cut Loaf in High Street, Orange Café in Obelisk Street, Penguin near St Tarcisius and the Sandhurst at Yorktown.[12] Above the jewellers in High Street in the 1960s was an Italian bar named Gallini's, Oasis and Virginian were

137 *The Old Manor café at Blackwater. Formerly a garage and roadside café with car sales and petrol, it became well known in the early 1960s as a meeting place for motorbike riders.*

on Osnaburgh Hill and the Zyder Zee was at Yorktown. All were warm and noisy but tame by comparison with the bikers' favourite, just over the bridge in Blackwater and known as the Old Manor. American-style diner Little Chef Number One opened opposite the Sandhurst Café in December 1962, although it was actually the second in the country, the first being at Reading. The original diner, with stools at the bar, was destroyed by fire in 1972 and a modern version erected on the same site.[13] Ladies could always enjoy afternoon tea at Betty Brown's, where the Misses Lindley served wonderful homemade cakes.

Music fans flocked to the Agincourt and the *Cambridge Hotel*. In 1963 at the Agincourt teenagers could dance to Johnny Kidd and the Pirates, Brian Poole and the Tremeloes, Billy J. Kramer, Gene Vincent,

The Searchers and The Hollies, and during one glorious week in August they could listen to the Swinging Blue Jeans and, two days later, Freddie and the Dreamers.[14] Buses were laid on to transport people back to their homes from this popular

138 *Rip Van Winkle, one of Bob Potter's acts, photographed on stage at the Agincourt singing 'Dinner with Drac' in March 1965.*

139 *Peter Sellers, with his wife Britt Ekland, attended a fundraising auction organised for a cancer charity by Camberley Round Table at London Road Recreation Ground in May 1965.*

venue, and soft drinks were available. In November 1963 the hall was taken over by Bob Potter, then a music impresario with recording studios at Mytchett.[15] He had travelled throughout the late 1940s and 1950s with his own band and by 1963 was managing a number of groups. None became famous, but The Bandits recorded music for Columbia, The Emeralds for HMV and The Dynamos for Pye records. In 1963 Frankie Vaughan opened the new

66 coffee bar in the High Street before signing copies of his record 'You're the One for Me' in aid of the National Association of Boy's Clubs. He then visited Solomon's showroom, were he sold tickets to win a new car, in aid of the local boys' Spartan Club.[16] Petula Clark was another regular visitor to town, opening the Cadet Corps Fete at Krooner Park and cutting the ribbon at the new Dyke's electrical store on the corner of Obelisk and Park Street in 1962. Well-known personalities opening fetes at London Road Recreation Ground included Harry Secombe and Peter Sellers.

In the 1950s there was a private zoo at Watchetts House. Mrs Wright had purchased a brown bear, monkeys and birds in the late 1940s when owner of the White Swan Laundry in Watchetts Road, and kept them in a row of garages opposite her business. During the war Watchetts had been requisitioned to accommodate Canadian troops, and in 1947 Mrs Wright purchased Watchetts House from the Over family. She applied to convert it for use as a guest house and private zoo. She was granted permission for six wire enclosures, and in 1949 applied to open the zoo to the public, who would be able to have afternoon tea and take boats out on the lake. Permission wasn't granted and the zoo was opened to friends and visitors on a non-paying basis.[17] In 1958 the estate was sold to developers Wickens of Chertsey, and the old house was demolished, the animals sold and Watchetts Lake Close built in its place. Today just the lake and one garden wall are left of what had been one of the largest estates in Camberley.

In addition to new social housing there was a massive expansion of private sector housing on the outskirts of town, primarily due to the planned motorway and the ownership of private cars. In July 1967 the Minister for Transport had finally made her decision on the route the M3 would take, following years of debate and a public enquiry. By October compulsory purchase orders were served on those affected by the new road. Only three houses were demolished, including Sollake Wood and Gladswood near the new Ravenswood roundabout.[18] Beaufront School would have been affected but had moved to Dorset when the motorway was proposed.[19] Work started on the section at the bottom of Prior Road in October 1968 and by April 1969 Brackendale Road and Waverley Drive were closed to through traffic. Concrete pillars for the bridge over Frimley Road were constructed by July 1969 and excavations near the former Royal Albert School were dug to a depth of nearly 40 feet.[20] In July 1974 the M3 from Sunbury to Lightwater was open for traffic and the section to Frimley was finished in 1975.[21]

The Goldney family, owners of Heatherside, were the first to see the potential of this new road. Sir Henry Goldney inherited the estate from his father in 1926. Prior to the Second World War he had planned to develop Heatherside as a housing estate; he gained consent for this although nothing came of the plan.[22] In June 1958 Goldney sold 98 acres of the estate, land from Goldney Road to The Maultway but not including the farm and surrounding fields,

to R.T. Warren for £45,000. In 1961 he sold the remaining 46 acres to Warren, including the nursery site and farm, for £75,000. Goldney justified the difference in price: 'In the first sale Warren had to bring the sewers across from Frimley Road up to The Maultway. Also the roads had to be continued on to The Maultway. All of these services I had the right to use. I was anxious to have this done so I calculated what it would cost and deducted it from what I considered the land was worth with all services connected.'[23] Work did not start on draining land until the spring of 1962. In July the first roads were built and by October Arundel Road and a section of Cumberland to Chobham Roads was complete. In December foundations for the first six houses in Cumberland Road were laid, although no further work took place until spring 1963 because of snow and frost. Work was also held up by Dr Barbara Moore not allowing drainage through her Eastlea Court Estate. The first house was completed by July 1963. Warren purchased Chobham House and Eden Wood in Upper Chobham Road that year and there were rumours he was to purchase Lytch Gate, Old Knowles and Winding Wood, giving him a frontage to the estate for some distance along the road. Nothing came of the plan and by June 1964 little further progress had been made. Mr Warren was now very ill and taking little part in the business. The vexed situation regarding the sewer and Barbara Moore rumbled on, and it was not until July 1965 that 12 houses were connected to it and residents were able to move in.[24] In October 1965 Leslie

140 *An aerial view of the partly built M3. The Frimley Road cuts through the centre of the photograph, with France Hill School and James Road estate on the left and the grounds of Frimley Park House to the right.*

King was able to report to Henry Goldney that 'all the houses in the Half Moon Pond area are occupied'.[25] In December Dr Moore attempted to disconnect the sewer and was imprisoned. The high profile case was covered by all the national papers.[26] In the spring of 1967 R.T. Warren was purchased by Bovis Group, who appointed local agents Sanderson & Co. to open an office in the High Street and advertise houses for £5,800 each.[27] In July 1967 Bovis sent in contractors to grub out the rhododendrons which grew along the Wellingtonia Avenue, and it was probably

114

just as well this fine avenue of trees was subject to a preservation order.

Schools, both within the estate and on the outskirts of it, were built to educate the growing number of children, Prior Heath opening in 1966 and Heather Ridge in 1967. Ravenscote and Tomlinscote opened for older pupils in 1972.[28] In late 1967 work in the Edgemoor Road area of Heatherside was continuing, and as the houses neared completion builders worked towards Brompton Sanatorium.[29] William King ran Heatherside Nursery until his death in March 1954 and his son, Leslie, continued the business until 1968 when, encroached on all sides by development, he decided to close it. Leslie wrote on 31 December 1968, 'Today is the official date for closing down the Nurseries. We are doing it very reluctantly and our regular customers are most upset.'[30]

Copped Hall, Tomlinscote, Warren and Alphington were sold and their extensive grounds became modern housing estates, providing new homes for young families but blurring the edges of the green corridor between Frimley and Camberley. Not all schemes went smoothly and developers at Copped Hall found it difficult to sell their houses. Copped Hall had been sold by auction on 15 April 1960 for £216,000 and by September work began to build the estate. Only thirty of the dwellings had sold by October 1962 as buyers considered them too close together and expensive at just over £5,000.[31]

Plans for a new Civic Centre on the east of Knoll Road, including a library, were proposed in October 1960.[32] The architects set the library back, 'to remove it from traffic and give it a quiet and pleasant setting', but this did not please the librarian, who wished to be by the road and, ideally, near shops.[33] It opened in 1964 and provided a spacious and well-stocked facility in comparison with the room behind the old Council Offices used since 1937. Camberley's first skyscraper, Victoria Court, described by developer Ron Best as a 'prosperity landmark', was built on the corner of London Road and Victoria Avenue in 1959. It was to be the first of many, which would 'become as familiar a feature of the Camberley face as they are of Manhattan'.[34] The Civic Hall was officially opened in Knoll Road on 1 October 1966 by the Earl of Munster, the Lord Lieutenant of Surrey.[35] In April 1968 Camberley was 'twinned' with Sucy-en-Brie, a town ten miles south-east of Paris. The first event between the towns was a football match which took place at Krooner Park in May.[36] In October of the same year Camberley Museum moved from its home at the Council Offices to Knoll Road, north of the library. More social housing was built in 1973, Sullivan and Gilbert Roads being named in honour of Sir Arthur Sullivan in the tradition of remembering those who had lived in the town or influenced its development.

A new road, Pembroke Broadway, was cut from Park Street to High Street, through the old railway goods yard. This required a row of shops to be demolished in Park Street, opposite Southwell Park Road, and cottages in Victoria and Albert Roads. A multi-storey car park was built here in 1971. For the first fortnight the Council offered motorists free parking in an attempt to encourage its use.[37] The car park was extended in 1983 when Ashwood House and the shops which currently include the Post Office were built.[38] The Victorian railway buildings, including the signal box in Heathcote Road, were demolished in 1975. Plans were passed in August 1976 for a new station and office block which was built by H.N. Edwards & Partners in 1977.[39] They were already considered ugly by 1979, when architect David Hutchinson described them as 'one of the best examples of thoroughly insensitive and inhuman scale that typifies so much of our growing town'.[40] In April 1974 the new Borough of Surrey Heath was formed, combining Frimley and Camberley Urban District with Bagshot Rural District Councils. It used the old Council Offices in both London Road and in Bagshot Green.

Sport and leisure facilities were in short supply as the town grew in size. The Blue Pool was taken over by F&CUDC in 1973

141 *Victoria Court was described as a 'prosperity landmark' when it was built on the corner of London Road and Victoria Avenue in 1959.*

but closed in 1976 due to the high cost of repairs.[41] An indoor pool had been planned for many years and numerous sites suggested before the decision was taken to use part of London Road Recreation Ground. The Arena Leisure Centre opened in 1984. The decision to build was taken in April 1981 after looking at the pool being erected in Farnham and agreeing to use the same design.[42] All did not go smoothly. The first builders chosen, Clayco of Farnham, were bankrupt by November 1982 and after a period of some months the contract to build was given to Wiltshire company W.E. Chivers.[43] With a 25 metre pool, an all-purpose hall and six squash courts, the Arena was the first council-owned leisure centre in the country to be run privately, by David Cross and John Staniland's Crossland Leisure Enterprises.[44] All-night cinema was introduced in 1972 in an attempt to lure people from their television screens. A 'Dracula Night' was held at the Classic, each member of the audience paying £1, a price which included a continental breakfast served at 4a.m. The cinema was about to be converted into three smaller screens and a bingo hall.[45] Rick Wakeman became Chairman of Camberley Football Club in 1983 and was associated with it until he left town to live on the Isle of Man.[46] Rick Wakeman was not the only pop musician to live in Camberley. Steve Brooks, formerly of The Jam, lived in Tekels Avenue in 1997, and Bros, who became teenage heartthrobs in 1988, were pupils at Collingwood School. The group, consisting of brothers Luke and Matt Goss and friend Craig Logan, was formed in 1984 and their first big hit, 'When Will I be Famous', was released in 1988. This was followed by two top-selling albums, *Push* in 1988 and *The Time* in 1989.[47] In 1997 there was another bout of pop-mania when Bob and Chris Herbert, former agents for Spice Girls and Bros, managed Five. In the documentary 'Neighbours from Hell', screened in March 1998, people from Heatherside estate were asked to comment on how bad it was having a boy band live near them in

Roxburgh Close. Five's debut single 'Slam Dunk' was released in December 1997.[48]

New estates were now being erected wherever a large house had stood, or on any available undeveloped land. Charles Church, the most prolific of all local builders, was born in Windlesham in 1943, the son of Charles Church of Broadway Road. The first property erected by Charles was a bungalow off Upper Chobham Road, which he built for his wife and family in 1965. He sold it and was able to purchase Oriel Hill

142 *An aerial view of Camberley looking south from the Staff College in 1979. The Staff Hotel stands on the corner of Park Street, next to some of the first houses built in the town, Hurst Wood and Staff Villas, which are screened by advertising hoardings just prior to their demolition*

143 *The view in 1979 looking north from Middle Gordon Road across town towards the Staff College. The new multi-storey car park and station are visible but office blocks in Pembroke Broadway and shops, including the Post Office in Princess Street, are still to be built.*

in Brackendale Road. He built four houses on this site, beginning a business which has developed properties throughout England. Charles Church Ltd was registered as a company on 14 March 1966. It built a reputation for designing houses in a traditional manner, the façades usually incorporating techniques from the past while the remainder of the structure was modern. His wife Susannah was responsible for much of the interior design. Charles

Church was passionately interested in flying and it was his love of this pastime that brought his life to an end in July 1989, at the age of 46, when his Spitfire came down in Hartley Wintney. His name lives on in the company that still proudly bears his name and occupies the offices built by him in Knoll Road. The Charles Church Band began life as the Camberley Silver Band on 4 November 1960 but changed its name to that of its sponsor in 1983.[49]

George Bryan Eden, who lived and worked in Camberley, was born in Guildford, where his father specialised in building Arts and Crafts houses. He started his career as works manager for Keil & Vevers in 1955. In 1963 he established his own company, G.B. Eden, initially in offices at 48 High Street and later in Park Street. When his wife Ruth died he set up the Eden Wildlife Trust in Kenya in her memory. The company built most of their homes in secondhand London stock bricks and examples of their work can be seen in Winding Wood Road and Crosby Hill.[50] Premier Properties was founded in 1982 by Roger Jelley and Roger Sterry and is perhaps the most active of current companies, with offices at Premier House in Tuscan Way.[51]

In 1974 Princess Anne and her husband Captain Mark Philips lived at Oak Lodge, within the grounds of the RMA.[52] With the bombing of Aldershot in February 1972, and the arrival of the royal couple, access to the grounds of the College was restricted and local families could no longer use it as a park. Camberley was not a major target, but it was vulnerable. In October 1985 a Staff College officer left his briefcase outside McDonald's in the High Street

144 *Charles Church, the Windlesham-born developer whose business was based in Knoll Road, Camberley, photographed with the Spitfire in which he lost his life in 1989.*

119

145 *The steel structure of the roof erected in 1989 over the 1970s shopping centre to make it more attractive.*

and Bomb Squad experts destroyed it. A second detonation took place the same week when a briefcase left in Knoll Road was destroyed,[53] and the following month a suspect package left on the doorstep of the Halifax Building Society was dealt with by remote control.[54]

The new town centre attracted good shops and offered a wide selection of produce but was not a place to linger, narrow streets creating a wind-tunnel effect and overhanging porticos allowing rain to drip onto shoppers. In January 1989 Phoenix Finance & Investments, a subsidiary of Mountleigh Group, started work on the transformation of the centre, including an additional thirty shops. The idea was to create the feel of a Victorian market hall, just thirty years after development had destroyed the Victorian town! A row of shops in the

146 *Main Square decorated for Christmas 1989 when the refurbishment of the centre was partly completed.*

High Street was demolished to create a new entrance and the centre was renamed Main Square in October 1991. For a few weeks a replica obelisk stood outside Boots store but, rather like Mountleigh, who went into administration the following year, it was short lived. Receivers were in control for two years until the development was purchased by Scottish Amicable in May 1994. It is currently owned by The Mall Group and is known as The Mall.[55] At the same time the multi-storey car park was refurbished and a second built in Knoll Road, and at the railway station end of the High Street a row of single-storey shops was demolished and a design-and-build competition held for new shops and leisure facilities on the corner of Pembroke Broadway.[56]

Surrey Heath House, designed by David Hutchinson and built by Lovells, was virtually ready for occupation on 15 June 1985 when disaster struck. A plumber working in the roof space triggered a fire which destroyed the roof and damaged much of the structure. The building was eventually opened by the Duke of Wellington on 17 July 1987. In 1993 a sculpture called 'Into our First World' was erected on the lawn in front of Surrey Heath House. Designed by Leicester artist Kenneth Ford, the design was inspired by the first of T.S. Eliot's four quartets, 'Burnt Norton'. Paid for by Windlesham firm BOC, it was unveiled by the Mayor of Surrey Heath, Jeanne Read, who had judged the competition for the design.[57] In

147   *The fire which broke out in June 1985, partly destroying the new Surrey Heath House.*

1997 it became a shrine to Diana, Princess of Wales, when flowers and poems were laid around its base and lanterns hung from the structure.

148 *Lanterns, photographs and flowers in memory of Diana, Princess of Wales, decorated the sculpture at the entrance to Surrey Heath House in 1997.*

The land between Park Street and Southern Road had been an area of housing. The original cottages in Upper and Lower Charles Street were demolished in 1963 and the hardcore used for the foundations of a car park.[58] In 1976, and again in 1985, it was proposed that a multi-storey car park be built here,[59] but in 1987 there were still 33 houses, 14 retail shops, almost 4,000 square feet of office space and the United Reformed church on the seven acre site. A Development Brief for the area[60] considered it a prime site for development, as 'the provision of major shopping floorspace in this area is seen by the Borough Council as the only realistic means of boosting to any significant degree the town centre's existing shopping in quantitative and qualitative terms'.[61] The Council already owned 30 per cent of

the land and by October 1988 compulsory purchase orders had been issued for the remainder, which was acquired at a cost of £17,000,000.[62] The development of the site was to be undertaken by Sheerwater Property Holdings, and be known as College Gardens. Planning permission was granted in August 1989. It was to have retail, community and leisure facilities including a new museum and almost 1,700 parking spaces. In June 1990, because of the economic situation at the time, Sheerwater shelved the project for a year.[63] The area was used as a temporary parking space from 1988, and after it was newly surfaced the Mayor of Surrey Heath officially opened what had become known as the 'nation's most expensive' car park in April 1994.[64] It was 1998 before developers THI came up with an alternative scheme, to include underground parking, a night club, fitness centre and shopping facilities, to be known as Park Place.[65] Over 3,000 people objected to the inclusion of a night club and it was 'called in' by the government, but in October 2000 John Prescott gave the green light.[66] The site has recently been developed, not by THI but by Crest Nicholson, who have included a substantial number of flats, lining the edge of the scheme along Southern Road, but no night club. The first shops opened in the spring of 2008, some twenty years after they were first proposed. All the earlier cinemas had closed when a new multi-screen facility in The Atrium opened on 14 November 2008.

Little is now left of the older firms. In 1975 control of Solomon's Garage had passed from Gerald and Trevor to their

149   *The temporary closure of Southwell Park Road, which took place in October 2007 to enable cranes to lift heavy material into the Atrium development.*

sons Alan and Ian. Another son, Robert, joined them in 1978, by which time they had additional premises in Lightwater and Doman Road. In 1988 they moved from the High Street to new headquarters in Yorktown, just off the new Meadows roundabout next to the *Lamb Inn*. Sadly, in November 1999 the business was declared bankrupt, 120 people lost their jobs and the administrators sold off the stock in an auction to raise the £200,000 owed to creditors.[67] Allders, originally James Page's shop, closed in April 2005 and part of the ground floor opened as a Farmer's Market on 14 November 2008. White's applied to move in 1953 from their garage on the west side of Knoll Road and London Road to the site of two former houses on the east

side.[68] Percy White retired in 1955 when his son Richard took over. He was followed by Percy's grandson Peter in 1974, and Peter's daughter Lindsay became MD in 1990. The

150   *The opening of a farmer's market in the old Allders Store in November 2008 has put to some use a building which had been empty since April 2005.*

123

151 *Camberley's Vue cinema on the day it opened in November 2008.*

business was sold to Martin's. Over's store is now occupied by Primark and the name is seen only on the side of removal trucks. With the opening of Tesco's and Marks & Spencer at The Meadows in 1989, and with traffic using the Blackwater Valley Relief Road, Yorktown has once again become a major shopping centre.

Camberley is still aware of its military background. Princes Harry and William have recently been trained for service at the RMA, when security was again heightened. Cadets can still be identified by their military bearing as they walk around the town, there is still a military tailor, and residents can enjoy the grounds of the Colleges on those rare occasions when special events are held there. The *Duke of York* is currently a sad shell, the *Staff Hotel* demolished, and the *Foresters* renamed *The Square*. France Hill remains as a road name but the school became Kings International in 2001. No town stands still. There will always be change, and controversy about that change, but to remove all the landmarks that give a town its unique heritage and make it like any town, anywhere, is to forget the reason for its existence. With only the grid-pattern left of his carefully zoned town, it is difficult to say whether Captain Charles Raleigh Knight would know where he was if he could see it now. At least he could visit the new Camberley Park and walk up the trail to the Obelisk, the only building to have been here when he purchased the land. He would see where cadets have engraved their initials in the stones, but probably never have known this had been a tradition since before he was a cadet. In 1801 a certain William Cobbett, visiting a relation in Frimley, had stopped here, 'where I spent an hour cutting my name in deep and large letters'.[69]

REFERENCES

Abbreviations used in references

BRO	Berkshire Record Office
CN	*Camberley News*
CRC	Church of England Record Centre
F&CUDC	Frimley and Camberley Urban District Council
NA	National Archive
RM&OG	*Reading Mercury and Oxford Gazette*
RMA	Royal Military Academy
SA	*Surrey Advertiser*
SHM	Surrey Heath Museum
SHC	Surrey History Centre

One FRIMLEY AND THE ROYAL MILITARY COLLEGE

1. Phil Stevens, *Surrey Heath in the Dark Ages* (Surrey Heath History Club, 1994).
2. Collection held at Surrey Heath Museum.
3. J.E.B. Gover, A. Mawer and F.M. Stanton, with A. Bonner, *Place Names of Surrey*, EPNS Vol. XI 1969.
4. John Blair, *Early Medieval Surrey* (1991).
5. Henry W. Aldred, *History of Frimley* (1896), p.3.
6. The inn stood near to where the concrete elephant stands today.
7. SHC G85/2/4 William Bray's diary of 1782.
8. The manor of Frimley would comprise Deepcut, Frimley, Frimley Green, Mytchett, Camberley and Yorktown today.
9. Major A.F. Mockler-Ferryman, *The Annals of Sandhurst* (1900), p.15.
10. Ibid. p.15.
11. Gordon Wellard, *The Story of Camberley 1798-1987* (198), p.11.
12. Phil Stevens, *Surrey Heath in the 18th Century* (2007), p.211.
13. NA Cres/2/42.
14. BRO DP/102/12/2.
15. Ibid.
16. SHC G85/2/4 William Bray's diary.
17. Centre for Kentish Studies U1590/C473/30.
18. NA WO1/943/65.
19. NA WO1/943/73.
20. RMA WO99/5/box7.
21. Ibid.
22. RMA WO99/33.
23. RMA WO99/5/box7.
24. RMA WO99/6.
25. RMAWO99/31.
26. Ibid.
27. Mockler-Ferryman, *Annals of Sandhurst*, p.18.
28. NA Cres/38/1978.
29. NA Prob1/23 Will of William Pitt.
30. Wellard, *Story of Camberley*, p.18.
31. G.B. Poulter, *History of Camberley* (1937).
32. SHC FRM/7/1.
33. RM&OG 9.8.1813.
34. SHM Lady Griselda Tekell letter 10.12.1815.
35. NA Cres/38/1978.
36. Ibid.
37. SHC QS/6/4/69 1826 copy of award.
38. RM&OG 27.11.1815.
39. SHC FRM/7/1 & 2589/2/4.
40. SHC QS/6/4/69 1826 copy of award.
41. SHC 6873/9 - a tax was levied on each window.
42. NA Maf20/79/1184.
43. SHC 6873/13.
44. SHC 2589/9/1.
45. SHC 2589/9/2c.
46. CN 12.12.1952.
47. Ken Clarke, *Time Gentleman Please*, p.23.
48. NA HO129/40.
49. Mary Bennett, *Frimley's Church of England Schools* (Surrey Heath History Club,1999), p.2.
50. SHC 2589/2/4.
51. Mary Bennett, *Faith in Frimley* (Surrey Heath History Club, 2000), p.26-9.

52. Ibid. p.28.
53. RM&OG 20.1.1834.
54. NA HO/44/26.
55. RM&OG 20.4.1833.
56. Vic Mitchell and Keith Smith, *Reading to Guildford - County Railway Routes* (Middleton Press, 1988) - the line opened in stages from 4 July 1849.
57. SHM Heather Toynbee's notes on Road and Rail.
58. SHM Sale catalogue Robert Cayley Campbell's property sold 13.5.1872.
59. RM&OG 21.7.1849.
60. Mary Bennett, *The Village Post* (Surrey Heath Museum, 2002), p.35.
61. SHM letter Hutchison 28.9.1970.
62. Arthur Lawrence, *Sir Arthur Sullivan Life, Story, Letters & Reminiscences* (James Bowden, 1899), p.234-7.

Two CAMBRIDGE TOWN AND THE DEVELOPMENT OF CAMBERLEY

1. RM&OG 22.5.1858.
2. NA Cres38/1978.
3. SHC 361/50/3.
4. A.R. Godwin-Austen, *The Staff and The Staff College* (Constable and Co., 1927), p.18.
5. Ibid.
6. Ibid. p.119.
7. RMA Records of the Royal Military Academy courtesy of Dr Peter Thwaites.
8. Army List 1842.
9. Army List 1846.
10. Burke's Landed Gentry 1868.
11. RM&OG 28.12.1861.
12. Ken Clarke, *Time Gentleman Please*, p.35 - *Staff Hotel* opened 1860, when four existing cottages were converted to a public house.
13. RM&OG 6.4.1861.
14. RM&OG 21.12.1861.
15. RM&OG 7.6.1862.
16. RM&OG 4.10.1862.
17. RM&OG 18.4.1863.
18. RM&OG 19.3.1864.
19. RM&OG 9.2.1867.
20. RM&OG 4.6.1870.
21. SA 15.5.1868.
22. RM&OG 18.1.1862.
23. IGI - birth 26.6.1859, and Cilgwyn records held at National Library of Wales.
24. NA Will of Benjamin Edward Hall ob6.12.1849 Prob. 11/2104/258.
25. SHC 748/1.
26. Probate Office Will of Cuthbert Collingwood Hall 1859/532.
27. SHC 748/1.
28. Ibid.

29. Ken Clarke, *The Royal Albert Orphanage & School* (Surrey Heath History Club, 2004), p.5.
30. RM&OG 18.1.1862.
31. R.A. Williams, *The London & South Western Railway* (David & Charles, 1973), p.71.
32. Ibid.
33. SA 29.10.1864.
34. SA 19.11.1864.
35. SA 2.9 and 7.10.1865.
36. RM&OG 10.3.1866.
37. This took the name Collingwood Mount by 1915.
38. SA 5.11.1864 and 26.11.1864.
39. SA 22.4.1865.
40. RM&OG 4.10.1862.
41. RM&OG 29.11.1862.
42. Williams, *London & South Western Railway*, p71.
43. Ibid.
44. Post Office Archives Post 35/368 Minute Book vol.161.
45. SHM Rail accidents file.
46. *Aldershot News* 18.1.1907.
47. Norman's Directory of Camberley 1889.
48. F&CUDC Rate Book April 1889.
49. SHM GDW notes Dr Attenborough.
50. Mary Bennett, *The Village Post*, p.21.
51. F&CUDC Rate Book April 1889.

Three CHURCHES, SCHOOLS AND THE URBAN DISTRICT COUNCIL

1. RM&OG 10.5.1851.
2. Ibid.
3. SHC Parish Registers for St Michael's.
4. Post Office Directory 1855.
5. CRC - Yorktown file.
6. Ibid.
7. Ibid.
8. SHM Sale Catalogue Auction 13.5.1872 at *Kings Arms*.
9. Anthony Macdermott, *The Church and Parish of St Tarcisius Commander* (Langhams Herald Press), p.11.
10. Kelly's Directory 1890.
11. CRC - Camberley file.
12. SHC 5271/4/18.
13. Today this building stands within the curtilage of St Paul's Church.
14. RM&OG 3.12.1881.
15. Mary Bennett, *Faith in Frimley*, p.48.
16. Ibid. p.47.
17. SHM St Michael's file.
18. SHM Congregational Church file.
19. Bennett, *Faith in Frimley*, p.50.
20. Kelly's Directory 1867.
21. Kelly's Directory 1890.
22. RG10/820/45.
23. 1901 census.

24. CN 20.2.1953.
25. F&CUDC Rate Book 1907 p.15.
26. SHM GDW - Michael Mortimer notes.
27. SHM - School files.
28. SHM Heather Toynbee's notes - education.
29. F&CUDC Minutes 5.10.1897.
30. Bennett, *Faith in Frimley*, p.51.
31. F&CUDC Minutes 2.1.1895.
32. Ibid. 5.2.1895.
33. CN 19.4.1929.
34. F&CUDC Minutes 23.4.1895.
35. Ibid. 24.4.1899.
36. Ibid. 4.5.1901.
37. The hospital was eventually moved to Frimley Green Recreation Ground where it served as a pavilion.
38. SHM Register of Property F&CUDC - land originally purchased 1883 and extended 1896.
39. F&CUDC Minutes 18.7.1905.
40. Ibid. 15.1.1907.
41. SA 25.9.1868.
42. SHM Diphtheria file - Mr W.H. Power's Report to the Local Government Board 7 April 1887.
43. George Bradnam, *The Old Brigade* (1985), p.1.
44. CN 13.7.1906.
45. SHM - Cottage Hospital file.
46. Ibid.
47. Ibid.
48. F&CUDC Minutes 20.9.1900.
49. Ibid. 4.5.1897.
50. Ibid. 29.9.1903.
51. Ibid. 2.2.1904.
52. SHM - Poulter file.
53. Mary Bennett, *Built to Last* (SHM, unpublished), p.2.
54. SHM - Poulter file.
55. F&CUDC Minutes 27.11.1906.

Four LEISURE IN A GROWING TOWN

1. F&CUDC Minutes 4.8.1896.
2. SHM Register of Property. F&CUDC 15.1.1898.
3. F&CUDC Minutes 6.12.1898.
4. Ibid. 27.6.1899.
5. SHM Register of Property F&CUDC .
6. SHM Recreation Ground file.
7. CN 15.6.1906.
8. F&CUDC Minutes 16.5.1901.
9. Ibid. 16.6.1902.
10. Ibid. 2.6.1903.
11. Ibid. 17.3.1904.
12. Ibid. 19.5.1908.
13. Drew's Directory 1907.
14. F&CUDC Minutes 21.4.1904.
15. SHM Football file - Vaughan deposit

16. CN 8.5.1931.
17. Ibid.
18. SHM Football file.
19. F&CUDC Minutes 17.3.1908.
20. Kelly's Directory 1903 - Drew's 1907.
21. Drew's Directory 1914.
22. SHM Golf Club file.
23. SHM reminiscences H. Cottrell, 1954.
24. Ibid.
25. F&CUDC Minutes 12.1.1904.
26. SHM Rumble's file.
27. CN 22.6.1906.
28. F&CUDC Minutes 26.9.1905.
29. SHM Ken Dawe's reminiscences. 22.2.1986.
30. CN 26.7.1929.
31. SHM Atkinson file.
32. SHM Valuation List.
33. SHM Muller file.
34. SHM Housing index.
35. NA Cres35/41.
36. SHC 748/1.
37. SHM Rate Book 1879.
38. SHM Collingwood Towers file.
39. SHM Frimley Park file.
40. SHM Obituary 1943.
41. SHM Abstract of Title 1951 Watchetts file.
42. SHM Whins file.
43. Minet Library.
44. SHM Abstract of Title - Alfred Ives 1909.
45. Macdermott, *The Church and Parish of St Tarcisius*, p.12.
46. Kelly's Directory 1882.
47. SHM Housing index.
48. SHM Doman File and 1871 Census RG10/820 folio 26.
49. CN obituary 16.2 1940.
50. SHM Valuation List.
51. Norman's Directory 1889.
52. Kelly's Directory 1890.
53. SHM Moorlands file AA352 and *Camberley News* June 1914.
54. Kelly's Directory 1867.
55. SHM Rate Book 1879 and Housing index.
56. SHM Sale catalogue Robert Cayley Campbell's property sold 13.5.1872.
57. CN obit 10.5.1929.
58. Mary Bennett, *Faith in Frimley*, p.47.
59. SHM Valuation List.
60. Mary Bennett, *Built to Last* (SHM, unpublished).
61. SHM Housing index.

Five OUTLYING ESTATES AND INFILL DEVELOPMENTS

1. SHM Yockley file.
2. He died 16.10.1904 and is buried at St Peter's.

3. Elaine Kimurray and Richard Ormond, *Sargeant* (Tate Gallery, 1998), p.18.
4. SHM Housing index.
5. SHC 748/1.
6. 1861 census RG9/430.
7. For a history of this nursery see Mary Ann Bennett, *Life and Work on Surrey Heath* (Phillimore, 2007), p.125-31.
8. SHM Frederick Street's diary.
9. Ibid.
10. Ibid. and Cadet Corps file.
11. SHM Edgemoor file.
12. SHM Housing index.
13. For a full account of house and school see Ken Clarke, *Ravenscote School* (1997).
14. SHM Tomlinscote file.
15. SHM Rate Book 1907.
16. SHM Sale Catalogue Tomlinscote.
17. *New York Times* online obituaries.
18. The history of this estate is recalled in Daisy Hills, *Old Frimley* (1978).
19. SHM Frimley Fuel Allotments file.
20. 1901 census RG13/609.
21. 1861 RG9/1143.
22. Hills, *Old Frimley*, p.88.
23. SHM Tekells Castle file.
24. 1871 RG10/820.
25. 1881 RG11/782.
26. SHM Heathcote House file.
27. SHM Valuation List.
28. SHM Housing index.
29. SHM Waverley and Belton files.
30. SHM George Abraham Grierson and Bihari Literature - Ashpa Gupta p.48.
31. SHM 1901 Rate Book.
32. SHM Tekells Ave - Abstract of title.
33. Online encyclopaedia of *Titanic* disaster.
34. Kelly's 1921 *Handbook to the Titled, Landed and Official Classes*.
35. NA BT31/31723/63174.
36. Ibid.
37. SHM Housing index.
38. Ibid.
39. F&CUDC Minutes 19.5.1901.
40. Graham Barson, *Camberley and Yorktown Between the Wars* (Sutton, 2007) p.61.
41. SHM France Hill Estate file.
42. SHM Housing index.
43. SHM Southwell Park Road file.
44. SHM Over's file.
45. SHM Pages file.
46. CN 7.5.1954.
47. CN 8.10.1974.
48. CN 14.8.1931.
49. CN 13.11.1937.

50. CN 20.5.1932.
51. Ibid.
52. SHM Housing index.

Six COLONELSTOWN AND RIBBON DEVELOPMENT

1. SHM Chancellor & Sons file.
2. General Gordon was in action at Omdurman and Atbara in Sudan in 1896.
3. Ooty was a hill station and Baroda a region in India.
4. CN 20.12.1930.
5. SHM VC files.
6. SHM Heather Toynbee's notes.
7. SHM Cattermole file.
8. Grave inscription St Michael's.
9. Ivy Potten, *Looking Back in Longing* (1985), p.75.
10. CN obituary 20.2.1931.
11. Kelly's Directory 1903 and Rate Book 1896.
12. Drew's Directory 1914.
13. *Aldershot News* 15.5.1925.
14. SHM Abbot Anderson file.
15. SHM St Michael's file.
16. SHM St George's file.
17. SHM St Tarcisius file.
18. SHM Housing Index.
19. Ibid.
20. Mary Bennett, *Faith in Frimley*, p.47.
21. SHM Housing index.
22. Mary Bennett, *Built to Last* (SHM, unpublished).
23. CN 22.8.1936.
24. SHM Rowlands file.
25. Reminiscences Tony Wells King.
26. Bennett, *Faith in Frimley*, p.50.
27. CN 27.8.1937.
28. SHM Reminiscences Edith Todd.
29. SHM Maywood file.
30. SHM Cordwalles file.
31. SHM GDW - Michael Mortimer notes.
32. Reminiscences Dr John Attenborough.
33. SHM GDW - Michael Mortimer notes.
34. In autumn 2004 the school moved to Birmingham.
35. SHM Blue Pool file.
36. CN 17.11.1922.
37. The original stand was destroyed in a fire in 1990 - CN 10.8.1990.
38. CN 29.11.1929.
39. CN 6.9.1929.
40. Drew's Directory 1907.
41. CN 1.1.1937.
42. CN 18.3.1938.
43. CN 26.11.1937.
44. SHM Camberley Heath file.

45. Drew's Directory 1914.
46. CN 5.4.1924.
47. Online - nationmaster.com/encyclopedia/Motocross.
48. SHM Choral and Orchestral Society file.
49. CN 14.10.1932.
50. Ibid.
51. CN 29.11.1929.
52. CN 2.1 1931.
53. SHM Cinema files.
54. CN 29.7.1932.
55. CN 29.1.1937.
56. CN 22.1.1937.
57. Ibid.
58. Peter Kay, *Steaming Through Surrey* (Middleton Press, 1986).

Seven THE SECOND WORLD WAR AND AFTER

1. CN 30.9.1938.
2. F&CUDC Minutes May 1939.
3. F&CUDC Minutes 25.9.1939.
4. Corinna continued as a pre-school nursery until 1986.
5. CN 2.6.1944.
6. CN January 1944.
7. CN May 1941.
8. F&CUDC Minutes 12.12.1944.
9. CN 16.7.1945.
10. CN August 1944.
11. SHM Obituary 1943 and Frimley Park file.
12. CN 12.2.1941.
13. CN 26.9.1941.
14. CN July 1942.
15. F&CUDC Minutes April 1942.
16. SHM Eastwoods file AA1079.
17. SHM Housing index.
18. SHM Linatex file - In 1954, they moved from their factory in Krooner Road to a building (designed by E.H. Eames) in Stanhope Road which is now demolished.
19. The factory closed in the late 1980s.
20. SHM Factory files.
21. SHM Red Cross files.
22. SHM Dorothy Worsley file.
23. SHM Dungay file.
24. F&CUDC Minutes February and March 1945.
25. F&CUDC Minutes April 1943.
26. CN 6.12.1942.
27. SHM Free French file.
28. SHM St Michael's file.
29. SHM Bombs and where they dropped file.
30. F&CUDC Minutes May 1945.
31. SHM Olympics file.
32. CN 13.2.1953.
33. SHM Shepherd file.

34. SHM Town development 1953.
35. SHM Old Dean files.
36. SHM Factory files.
37. Ibid.
38. Reminiscences of Ron Francis.
39. SHM Old Dean files.
40. SHM Highwayman file - closed 1988 after a riot and demolished September 1990.
41. SHM Catholic church file.
42. SHM St George's file.
43. SHM St Martin's file.
44. CN 21.6.1957.
45. 1971 census figures.
46. CN 31.1.1964.
47. SHM Town Centre Development files.
48. SHM A&N file.
49. SHM Town Centre Development files.
50. Ibid.
51. SHM France Hill School file.
52. SHM School files.
53. CN 20.2.1953.
54. SHM School files.
55. CN 7.1.1975.
56. CN 28.1.66.
57. CN 20.3.1979.
58. SHM Hillside file.
59. SHM Natural History Society file.
60. SHM Maxwell night file.
61. SHM Lodge file.
62. SHM Camera Club file.
63. Tony Wells King.
64. SHM Camberley Cricket Club archive.
65. SHM Maclagan file.
66. SHM Lucky 7 file.

Eight THE MODERN TOWN

1. SHM Kate Ward file.
2. CN 18.10.1968.
3. SHM CN undated cutting (1950s).
4. SHM Camberley Beetle file - official report.
5. SHM Rabies file - report 14.10.1969-11.3.1970.
6. CN 17.7.1970.
7. SHM Concrete Elephant file - notes by Hazelle Jackson.
8. SHM Trollope & Colls file 23.6.1964.
9. CN 12.11.1982 and 6.11.1987.
10. SHM Chas McDevitt file and Tony Wells King.
11. CN 3.5.1974.
12. Tony Wells King.
13. SHM Little Chef file.
14. CN March-September 1963.
15. CN 8.11.1963.
16. CN 1.11.1963.
17. SHM Watchetts file.
18. SHM M3 file.
19. SHM School file.

20. SHM King letters, Goldney papers.
21. CN 12.7.1974.
22. SHM Housing index 21.10.1938.
23. SHM Goldney papers.
24. Ibid.
25. SHM King letters - Half Moon Pond area is Arundel Road.
26. SHM Barbara Moore file.
27. SHM King letters.
28. SHM School files.
29. SHM King letters.
30. Ibid.
31. Ibid.
32. CN 7.10.1960.
33. Ibid.
34. CN 18.9.1959.
35. SHM Civic Hall file.
36. Local Affairs Magazine (F&CUDC, 1968-9).
37. CN 30.7.1971.
38. CN 13.5.1983.
39. CN 17.5.77.
40. CN 6.2.1979.
41. SHM Blue Pool file.
42. CN 16.4.1981.
43. SHM Arena file.
44. CN 12.10.1984.
45. CN 23.6.1972.
46. SHM Wakeman file.
47. SHM Bros file.
48. SHM Five file.
49. SHM Charles Church file.
50. SHM Eden file.
51. Mary Bennett, *Built to Serve* (SHM).
52. SHM Princess Anne file.
53. CN 22.10.1985.
54. CN 19.11.1985.
55. SHM Town Centre Development files.
56. SHBC Camberley Town Centre Sub-Committee 19.11.1990.
57. SHM Into our First World file.
58. CN 24.4.1963.
59. CN 26.10.1976 and 29.10.1985.
60. John Silvester published November 1987.
61. Development brief John Silvester (November 1987).
62. SHBC Town Centre Sub-Committee 19.11.1990.
63. CN 2.6.1990.
64. SHM LWPS file.
65. CN 10.4.1998.
66. CN 2.11.2000.
67. CN 12.11 and 17.11.1999.
68. CN 29.3.1953.
69. CN 18.7.1978. This is not the William Cobbett of *Rural Rides*, although the Frimley and Farnham Cobbetts are believed to be related.

INDEX